Victorian London

Graham Norton

Picture sources: Metropolitan Police Gazette, 76;
Radio Times Hulton Picture Library, cover, 15, 20,
21, 34, 44, 45, 54, 57, 61, 70, 74, 80, 94, 96, 98,
104, 108, 113, 114. Photographs in centre section:
Radio Times Hulton Picture Library, 3, 4(a) and
(b); Michael Taylor, 1, 2, 5, 6, 7, 8.

Macdonald & Co. (Publishers) Ltd.

First published in 1969 by
Macdonald & Co. (Publishers) Ltd.,
St. Giles House, 49 Poland St., London W.1

Made and printed in Great Britain by
Purnell & Sons Ltd., Paulton, Somerset

Discovering London 8

Victorian London

Graham Norton

Macdonald : London

Contents

Cover: Victorian East Enders on Bank Holiday.

Introduction

The London we live in today is overwhelmingly a Victorian creation. This book, the last in the *Discovering London* series, is a small act of homage to our great-grandparents, and to their fathers and mothers, who lived, and sometimes suffered, in a great experiment of mass urbanisation.

Out of their living laboratory emerged the rules of health which every city must observe today. They also raised a city to be proud of, a capital not only of the richest nation in Europe, but of the greatest Empire that had yet been seen. They believed in themselves. In their confidence they put up buildings that immediately became symbols of the power and might of their capital, such as the Houses of Parliament and Tower Bridge.

They would have scorned the idea that this nation's independence would ever be qualified, that in matters of finance we should ever be the client-state of another. They knew their own minds. We may dislike some of their buildings—but there is never anything half-hearted about them, and even their ugliness can inspire a wry affection. Placed alongside the characterless commercial office blocks of today, the qualities of Victorian buildings become very apparent.

The Victorians built many of the houses we live in, the theatres, the great assembly halls and parks we visit in our leisure time, the streets and railways we travel along. Indeed, so much of 19th-century London is our London that, unlike earlier volumes, this book makes no specific suggestions on places to visit, though it cites numerous surviving monuments of the Victorian age; these the enthusiastic reader can find for himself in or near the area in which he lives or works. Similarly, the list of men and women who contributed to Victorian London is so vast that it would be invidious to select only a few. The Who's Who in earlier books has therefore also been omitted.

I should like to thank Mr. A. T. Gore, Principal Statistician, Greater London Council, for his advice on London's population; Marion Giordan, for allowing me to draw on her store of knowledge of Victorian customs and Victorian structures in London; and Mr. A. R. Byers for information on the Victorian theatre. Mr. G. Perry read the text and made a number of helpful suggestions.

Capital of the World

Victorian London was the biggest city the world had ever seen. At the old queen's death it was also the metropolis for the largest and most extensive empire known to the history of man. It surpassed in population most of the dominions of the queen, and many of the states of Europe. If the world itself had a capital, this was it. For not only, as the British Empire itself grew, became ordered and consolidated, did London become the Imperial capital, hub of Empire, the law-giver, it was also the centre for the whole elaborate structure of the 19th-century world.

If money talks, then London could shout the loudest in Queen Victoria's day. In the vaults of the Bank of England sat far more gold bars than in any other country. The gold sovereign was far more common than the paper pound note, and was accepted all over the world. But the sober men in the City were unlikely to shout. They were soft talkers, pillars of middle-class propriety, at least on the surface. London had become the world's unchallenged centre for banking, commerce and finance. With the money the City commanded, Britain was networked with railways, the world girdled with steamship routes and cables, America developed and opened up.

Middle-class values—sobriety, thrift, cleanliness, and above all probity—these were the ideas which dominated Victoria's England. During the three-quarters of a century that she reigned, they were increasingly applied to all classes of society. The open raffishness of the aristocracy in the Regency period was curbed or went underground (hence the frequent references to Victorian hypocrisy) and the filth and squalor, the unbelievable poverty in which the less fortunate working class lived were at least partially tackled. The Reform Bill of 1832 had put the old ramshackle system of franchise on a reasonably rational basis, one that was eventually to be expanded to include working-class men—but not women, of any class—in the electorate by 1884. The Houses of Parliament are a palace put up by the Victorians—their most splendid structure in all London, all England—to demonstrate, not only to the nation, but also to the world, the triumph of ordered, parliamentary liberty.

For, by and large, Victorian England had a way of life which it considered infinitely exportable. Everyone believed in progress, that man could solve all his problems. The triumphs of engineering—British engineering—were visible evidence of man's progress in conquering his environment. And on the social and political front, constitutional monarchy had presided over the changes from the 18th century onwards which had made Britain the most powerful and the richest country in the world. Liberty, free speech, a free press, the rule of law—these were the envy of less fortunate nations.

'Do as we do' was Britain's message to the world. And throughout Europe, with often open support from British governments (but not always from Queen Victoria), constitutional liberal revolutionaries worked for the establishment of democratic rule. By 1900, it would seem on the surface that the political Englishing of Europe at least was complete. There were constitutional monarchs (most by this time related to Queen Victoria—she and Albert had restocked most of the royal houses of Europe) and representative governments almost everywhere. Some of this constitutionalism was deceptive; it was then thought necessary for a nation, particularly a new one, to have a parliament, just as today small African states demand that latest status symbol, a national airline.

In the Empire, the same pattern followed. At the beginning of Victoria's reign, the colonies were largely scattered and small, ports of call on the trade routes so vital to Britain's commercial supremacy. India was a special case, an empire in itself, nominally run until 1858 by a private concern, the East India Company. The company's territory was only a small portion of what we know as India, and its position where it did not directly rule was secured by treaties with the neighbouring native states, a system which, with modifications and extensions, continued when the British government assumed greater responsibility. But in the colonies populated by settlers from the United Kingdom, it was assumed that self-government and probably eventual independence would come about, just as it had done in America. To some politicians, they were 'wretched millstones around our necks', as they were to the young Disraeli. Most of Britain was later to change its mind, just as he did, and from the Queen's Golden Jubilee, became unabashedly Imperialist. More and more self-government was given to the white colonies, but this only seemed to strengthen their attachment to Britain and its queen.

As well it might—for the power of Britain alone could defend them, provide the best market for their products, and the finance they needed. The British fleet was the largest in the world. The British army was one of the smallest in Europe, but it was designed largely for fighting small colonial wars, little more than police actions. We relied on the Navy to keep the continental armies penned up, to police the waterways of the world and to keep trade free. The Admiralty in Whitehall was something of a world police station, Downing Street the judge, and Westminster a grand jury, a court for the trial of the world's affairs.

Never before had so much been concentrated in one place. There were astounding collections of books—it was to the great library of the British Museum that Karl Marx came to write *Das Kapital*, the bible of communists everywhere; of pictures, many of which could be found in the private collections of great noblemen, whose town houses, miniature palaces, were still standing in Park Lane and the West End even at the close of the century; and of course it was where the literary giants, Thackeray, Trollope, above all Dickens, could be found. The great city itself was the raw material of many of their novels.

It was a centre for science, for engineering, for medicine (here Lister pioneered antiseptic surgery), for the most obscure study that could be thought of. The odd characters who appear throughout the Sherlock Holmes stories were to be found in real life in 19th-century London.

London was also a place of refuge. It was here that the persecuted came to seek freedom from oppression. To London came, as plaques in obscure streets sometimes testify, men like Mazzini, Garibaldi, Kossuth. And, more numerous than the political refugees came the victims of racial persecution, the Jews, fleeing the pogroms of the tsar. They formed the biggest number of foreign-born Londoners by the end of the century in a city that was now essentially cosmopolitan: in 1900 there were an estimated 30,000 Germans, 15,000 Americans (100,000 were thought to visit London each year) and more Irish than in Dublin.

Expansion

Above all, London *grew*. The administrative county of London (the old London County Council area) had 1,949,000 people in 1841. (Censuses are taken every ten years after they first began, in 1801.) In 1901, the year of Queen Victoria's death, there were 4,537,000 Londoners. And that last figure, if everybody in the outer suburbs of 'Greater London' was included, would rise to over 6½ million people.

Some of that increase was due to the rise in the birth-rate. But a large part of the increase was accounted for by immigrants from the country districts and provincial towns, and from Scots and Irish coming to London in the hope of bettering themselves (or, in the case of many from Ireland, to escape from famine when the potato crops failed).

There was a huge demand for domestic servants. Half London's population seemed at one time to be serving the other; in the homes of the middle-class, usually even the least prosperous business family could afford a maid, so the number of young girls who came into London was huge. The biggest jump in migrant population came in the years 1851–61. In those ten years, 337,000 young women and 241,000 young men between the ages of 15 and 24 came to London. It was the railways—then for the first time effectively covering the country—which brought them, and also made it possible to transport the food, the coal, and all the other necessities of life for such a concentration of population.

What sort of city was it then that the Archbishop of Canterbury, the Prime Minister, Lord Melbourne, and the members of the Accession Council dashed through on June 20, 1837, to see the new queen at Kensington Palace? The city was, of course, the product of many continuous years of habitation, since Roman times. It had grown outwards from the historic City of Guildhall and St. Paul's, as necessity required, with almost no attempt at planning. After the Great Fire of 1666 Sir Christopher Wren produced a master plan for the City, which would have produced an accessible and uncramped centre, but the City Fathers insisted on going back as far as possible to the twisting alleys that were there before. These medieval roads and tracks, and their counterparts in the villages that London swallowed up in the 18th and early 19th centuries, became the roads of Victorian London, suffering the immensely swollen traffic and causing far longer delays in traffic jams than we know today.

Until 1837 London had grown largely from east to west, and mostly on the north shore of the Thames. The river provided one means of getting about, and already by this time the small boats were being driven out by small steamships. Two months before Victoria's accession, steamers carrying 120 passengers at a time ran every 15 minutes between London Bridge and Westminster Bridge, all day from 8 am to 9 pm. Greenwich and Woolwich were also well served, and it was possible to work in Whitehall or in the City and return to these areas at night.

Transport

The roads had hardly been widened since the middle ages, including the main east-west thoroughfares. These are best described in the words of a Guide to London of 1851: 'They lead from either side of Hyde Park to the Bank, and then fork off again, and terminate in the remote east side of the metropolis, forming a design somewhat in the shape of an hour-glass.' Along these routes omnibuses—which had originated in Paris—had been plying since 1829. They were usually drawn by two horses (the City streets were too narrow to allow more) and they carried between 12 and 15 passengers at a 6*d*. fare. There were no bus stops; passengers shouted out when they wanted to be put down. The bus would also swing over to the other side of the road and drop you at

14

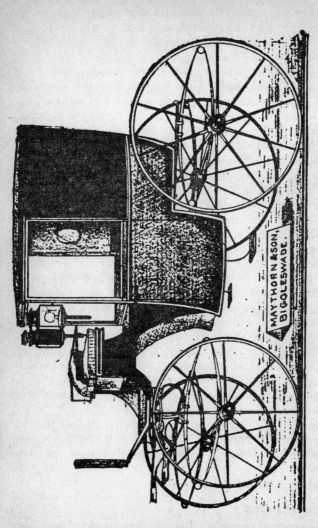

A brougham, one of several horse-drawn vehicles hired out by livery stables or used by private owners.

MAYTHORN & SON, BIGGLESWADE.

15

a house or shop on the right-hand side if you liked—a service appreciated by ladies, as skirts swept the ground, and the roads were covered with filth, of which the most savoury was horse-dung dropped by the thousands of animals.

But the first buses were not for the workers, who could not afford such fares. They were mainly for merchants and superior clerks, or people with small independent incomes. The upper classes and the rich City men had their own carriages, and there were also cabs, 'hackney carriages', although these were often not very fashionable vehicles; many were second-hand gentlemen's carriages, with sagging springs and staggering wheels.

The first London railway had arrived: it was the London and Greenwich, the first section of which, from Deptford to Spa Road, Bermondsey, opened in February 1836; the line was at London Bridge by December of the same year. This was to become the first of the great suburban stations, and many other lines were afterwards run into it and the station enlarged. The line ran through an area of market gardens (all built on well before the end of Victoria's reign) but was raised above the ground on an arched viaduct, a method much copied by subsequent constructors, as you can see almost anywhere today. 'Railway arches' became a feature of our urban landscape; they also had their uses, either to the railway company for storage space and small workshops, or to local tradesmen. The London and Greenwich was even able to lease one arch as a public house.

In 1837 the first of our present day main-line stations was opened. This was Euston, for the London and Birmingham railway; however, in that year, the line reached only to Boxmoor, and Birmingham was only reached in the following year.

Overcrowding

These were all signs of what was very quickly happening

16

to London. But, exciting as they are, the railways, the omnibuses and the steamers must not obscure the true fact that most people walked. This in itself meant that it was necessary to live pretty close to the job, particularly as workers, in factories or small workshops, started work very early, at dawn in many cases. By today's standards there was intolerable overcrowding. In such districts as Whitechapel, Holborn and Lambeth there was almost no sanitation. Typhus, cholera (from which 5,000 died in 1832) and all kinds of fevers were commonplace. In 1838 a count of workhouse population shows that out of 77,000 people, one-fifth had caught 'fever', and 1,300 had died of it. There was very little main drainage or sewage. Most houses were built over cesspools, some so huge that they became nothing less than cess-lakes. Houses were built back-to-back, side-to-side, anyway so long as they could be fitted in. There were numerous cul-de-sacs, small stifling courts and alleys over which tenement houses loomed. In 1840 a Select Committee of the House of Commons heard a witness say : 'At present there is no more regard paid in the construction of houses to the health of the inhabitants than is paid to the health of pigs in making sties for them. In point of fact, there is not so much attention being paid to it.'

There was even a tax on windows, which was not repealed until 1851 (what the Crystal Palace would have had to pay otherwise!); this resulted in passages, cellars and stairs being left entirely without ventilation. 'A tax upon light and air, a tax more vicious in principle and more injurious in its practical consequences than a tax upon food.'

The real horrors of cholera and smallpox descended on London in the 1840s, and were so dreadful that at last the task was taken in hand. The effect of terrible overcrowding and of living in filth, of physical squalor and the resulting reduction of human beings to a near-animal state, these were already known. There were two

Londons, that of the rich and comfortably off, and that of the poor. As members of the House of Commons were told in 1838, there were districts of London 'through which no great thoroughfares passed, and which were wholly occupied by a dense population composed of the lowest class of persons, who, being entirely secluded from the observation and influence of better educated neighbours, exhibited a state of moral degradation deeply to be deplored'.

Buildings

The better off had gone west, first to the West End, and then further still. In the late 18th century rich noblemen laid out their London estates as residential areas, in elegant squares and crescents. The Dukes of Bedford did in Bloomsbury, the Portlands in their estates north of Oxford Street. Mayfair was converted into a fashionable district. Then, in Victoria's infancy, Regent Street was cut, and Regent's Park was lined with imposing terraces.

Regency builders put up tall terraces, which contained in their separate houses extensive establishments of servants and children for the well-to-do. Bricks were out of scale in such grand buildings, and so stucco, cement covered with paint, hid the bricks beneath. All kind of ornament was introduced—mainly Greek and Roman in derivation, but sometimes Egyptian or 'Gothick'. The villas in Regent's Park West are good examples of this mixture of inspirations and they are also interesting in that some of them are semi-detached. They were the first in London, and it was here that for the first time in London, or in any other English town, the terrace was abandoned for the 'semi'—which became the pattern for the vast Victorian suburbs not only of London, but of every city and town in Britain.

It was, however, mainly in terraces of stucco that London grew in the first years of Victoria's reign. The drift westwards had now reached what was called at the time 'Tyburnia'. This area, built up from the later 1830s to 1850s, took its name, rather surprisingly from Tyburn Tree (now Marble Arch) and comprised what we know as Bayswater, Paddington and North Kensington. A walk in this area, particularly around Sussex Gardens or Stanhope Street, will give a good idea of the sort of houses the 'omnibus trade' lived in. These tall, imposing houses were afterwards also built in South Kensington, and later still a debased variety was to follow in Earls Court. Some of them became, and remained, the residences of the grander sort of people for which they were intended. But some, particularly those put up in the 1860s in the Notting Hill Gate area, almost immediately became what they are today—tenement houses, the best rooms on the first floor being let as a suite, and the servants' rooms in attic and basement going to young people making their way in the city, or to the old, lonely and failing.

Food

The London of 1837 still depended very much on local food supplies, as the national network of railways was yet to come. Milk came from cows quartered all over London, and hens, even pigs and sheep, were kept quite close to the centre. Above all there were the famous market gardens of such places as the 'Jerusalem Land', extending along the flat alluvial bank of the Thames between London and Greenwich, and all about Fulham, Battersea, Chelsea, Putney and Brentford. These gardens were intensively fertilised with horse manure from the stables and streets, and the droppings of the cows in the metropolitan dairies; the same carts which took loads of cabbages and peas to Covent Garden returned richly laden with dung.

Hideously, vast quantities of animals were crudely slaughtered at Smithfield, or at private slaughter-houses,

Church Lane, St. Giles (about 1840), part of the overcrowded 'Rookery', which was swept away in the 1880s.

A scene at Covent Garden market, which expanded enormously in Victorian times to supply London's ever-growing population.

for which no licence was necessary, often situated in foetid cellars in the heart of the slums. The groaning tables we see on Victorian Christmas cards were furnished with meat much of which would be condemned by a modern sanitary inspector merely on suspicion of point of origin.

We can be sure none of these thoughts entered the minds of the figures converging on Kensington Palace that June morning in 1837, the first of the new reign. The surroundings there were pleasant—besides the glorious Park itself, the whole area was one of a small 'court suburb', a smart village clustering around the old church and the High Street which led into London. The shops catered for the surrounding houses, many with extensive grounds of an acre or two, which belonged to the aristocracy or the very rich. The site now occupied by the Albert Hall was Gore House, a centre of fashion and intrigue. There was Holland House, originally Jacobean, the headquarters of the Hollands and the Foxes, leaders of a powerful clan in the Whig party. Slightly to the south of the High Street were other houses, standing up amid the nurseries and market gardens: Gloucester Lodge, Colherne House, Brompton Park, while at Earls Court there was a large farm and the remains of a fortified mound. Beyond, there lay open country, the rich farmland of an England which was also the most advanced farming country in the world, cultivated by the most scientific methods. The farms, protected by tariffs, particularly the Corn Laws, fed rich rents into the bank accounts of the traditional aristocracy. That elite was now intermarrying with the manufacturers of the industrial north, just as it had done with City bankers and West Indian planters. The British social system could absorb all changes given time.

And so they gathered, confident men who had ridden the storm of the Napoleonic Wars and the internal troubles that had followed them, curious to see the latest sprig of an ancient monarchy, which for the last forty years had largely distinguished itself by scandalous behaviour.

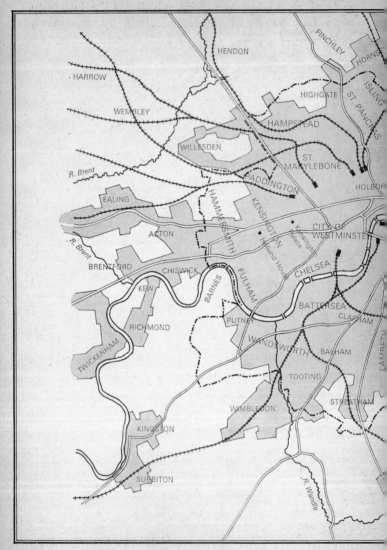

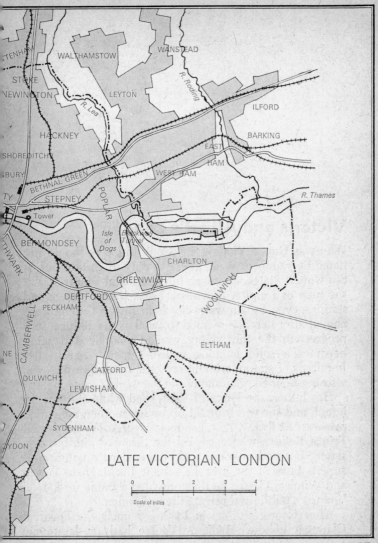

LATE VICTORIAN LONDON

0   1   2   3   4

Scale of miles

25

Victoria and Albert's London

Who was Queen Victoria anyway? And why should her name be stamped on an age, not only in Britain but in the United States, and even in continental countries. On the map of Empire, provinces, lakes, towns, streets and stations, even a giant water-lily from British Guiana were named after her. She seemed to swell as the 19th century progressed; the tiny young woman who liked dancing becomes a solid looming figure, seldom seen in her hundreds of statues without orb, sceptre and tiny crown, a strong-minded grandmother to the world.

Her father, the Duke of Kent, died while she was an infant, and she was brought up by her mother, a German princess. At first, it was her uncle George IV, the famed Prince Regent, who occupied the throne. Vain, fat, corsetted, but with a warm and compassionate nature and superb taste in the arts, he rebuilt Buckingham Palace and Windsor Castle; he thus provided a frame for Queen Victoria's public and private life in London.

After George's death in 1830, her uncle the Duke of Clarence became William IV. He had no legitimate children, and so Victoria became heir to the throne. The next in line was an unpopular uncle, the Duke of Cumberland, who became the king of Hanover, since Victoria, being a woman, could not rule there. The two thrones thus separated.

Victoria was popular from the beginning of her reign. She was such a contrast to her uncles, who, in spite of their mistresses, were no longer glamorous or attractive figures. She gave an image of purity to the monarchy which it had not had for many years. She was also determined to work hard and be worthy of her duty: 'I will be good', she promised. The rights and powers of a constitutional sovereign, particularly in a time of constitutional change, were not easy to convey to a girl of eighteen. Lord Melbourne, the Prime Minister, was able to do this by and large. He was perhaps a little too successful in establishing ascendancy over her. Once, out riding in London, the queen was jeered at with shouts of 'Mrs. Melbourne'.

Prince Albert

She was thrown into politics right away, for in those days the death of a sovereign always meant a general election. However, she began to acquire judgment by experience. In 1840, she married Prince Albert of Saxe Coburg-Gotha. He was her cousin, although there has been some speculation that he was not in fact the son of the Duke of Coburg, but of his mother's reputed lover, a partly-Jewish chamberlain.

Whatever may have been Albert's ancestry, he was a most remarkable man, and his effect on Victoria was profound. His interests were wide-ranging: science, art, politics, particularly international affairs, he threw himself into all these activities with immense enthusiasm. At first he was not generally welcomed in England, particularly as it was thought that he was trying to rule the country through the queen, and thus to usurp the functions of elected ministers. This fear was in time shown to be largely groundless, as Albert became more influential and appreciated.

In particular, the prince left his impression on the appearance of London. The first of the public tasks he undertook in his own right was to chair a Royal Commission. This was to meet in March 1842 to 'take into consideration the Promotion of Fine Arts in this country, in connection with the Rebuilding of the Houses of Parliament'. (The old Palace of Westminster had been largely destroyed by fire in 1834 and the House of Commons and the House of Lords were accommodated in the patched-up portions of the ruins, together with a number of other public bodies that had previously had a home there.) In 1836 Charles Barry won a public competition to rebuild the new Palace, offering a design in the 'Gothic' style. (There were many other designs—97 were entered—and some of them can be seen on the walls of various rooms in the Palace of Westminster.) However, hardly anything had been built by the time Prince Albert's commission had begun to sit.

The prince also urged that a new wing be built to John Nash's Buckingham Palace. As built for George IV, it faced the Mall, consisting of an open courtyard with projecting pavilions, all elegantly colonnaded. Now this was closed up with a new east wing, which is the front of the present palace. The rooms behind the façade are those put up by Albert, but the actual frontage itself is 20th-century, since the work of Albert's architect, Blore, was so undistinguished that it had to be replaced.

Albert's greatest legacy was the Great Exhibition of 1851, the Crystal Palace and the South Kensington museum complex which, though mostly erected after his death, owed much to him. His part in all this will be told in a later chapter.

Queen Victoria meant much to the Victorians, and is of

great interest to us, because she exactly reflected so much of what they did, thought, or were themselves interested in. As they changed, so did the queen, in an almost uncanny way. She mirrored life—and life also took cues from her. She shared with Albert a great curiosity about life in her kingdom—though it was Albert who was the pioneer, who tried things out and then reported back. He was a great broadener of the queen's interests. Almost as soon as they married, he was riding on the railway. The queen herself did not undertake this new form of locomotion until 1842, when she travelled from Slough to Paddington in 25 minutes. Soon afterwards, a Royal Train was ordered (its carriages can be seen in the Transport Museum at Clapham). The royal couple took up photography as early as 1842, and there is a great collection of their photographs at Windsor. They sketched, they wrote, they travelled, visiting museums, art galleries, antiquities and country-houses, and they took an interest in the condition of the very poor. They admired scientific invention; Queen Victoria took advantage of the invention of anaesthetic gas during childbirth, and thus set an example to the other mothers of the country.

After Albert's death, in 1861, she was desolate, and for years became the 'Widow of Windsor', keeping out of the public eye. In her duties as head of state she was as industrious as ever, at least in the matter of reading state papers and keeping a close eye on the doings of her ministers. From this seclusion she emerged in her later years as the Great White Queen Over the Water, mother of Empire. Under Disraeli's encouragement she took her imperial duties seriously, learning Hindustani (though with a very limited vocabulary) and building on an Indian Hall to Osborne House in the Isle of Wight. Victoria's children (nine altogether) married into the royal houses of Europe, though Bertie, the Prince of Wales, later Edward VII, was a disappointment. From

29

his teens he enjoyed the company of women and of less restrained circles than Albert and Victoria would have liked. It was Edward who presided over London 'society' in the 1880s and 1890s, when mention of the 'Marlborough House set' would send a tremor of disapproval through any gathering of the ultra-respectable.

Trains and Drains

Two features dominated the London of the 1840s—trains and drains. We have already seen that Euston Station and London Bridge were established before Victoria came to the throne. The Great Western had a line into Paddington by 1838, although it was not the station we know today. In the east, the Eastern Counties Company ran from Mile End to Romford in 1839, and established a terminus at Shoreditch in 1840. (The present Bishopsgate Goods Depot occupies the site.) In the same year the London and Blackwall railway ran a line from the Minories, just outside the city, to a pier at Blackwall.

In the south, a line running from Wimbledon and Clapham to Nine Elms was pioneered by the London and Southampton Railway. This line was extended to Waterloo in 1848, and eventually became the London and Brighton railway (Brighton was reached in 1841), running its services into Waterloo.

The London and Blackwall at first used a system of continuous cables and stationary steam engines (abandoned in the later 1840s and replaced by locomotives).

Cables were also used at Euston. Here the trains were faced with a steep gradient, further complicated by the need to carry the trains over the Regent's Canal. Locomotives were therefore detached at Camden, and the carriages were drawn into Euston station by cable. The great bank of earth which was put up by the engineers to maintain the gradient of 1 : 330 into Camden can still be seen, and the locomotive depot is still there too. Camden Town is a splendid place in which to see the works of the railway age of the 1840s. The goods yard in Chalk Farm Road is honeycombed with tunnels, which were used to bring the horses from their stables. These were an important adjunct to the railway, taking goods to and from the stations (and even drawing special buses carrying passengers transferring from one terminus to another across London). These stables are now used by Gilbeys, the gin manufacturers. It is possible to get in and explore this relic.

The Round House

But the most impressive monument to the Railway Age in Chalk Farm Road is the Round House, a huge circular building, which can be seen both from the road and from passing trains and which now houses Arnold Wesker's Centre 42. It was devised as a turn-table house for locomotives; here they were turned around, inspected, and prepared for the journey north again. It was built in 1847, and was designed by Robert Stephenson, son of George, who built the Stockton to Darlington railway and was the pioneer of practical railways. The Round House has a huge roof of Welsh slate supported by 24 cast-iron columns, with enormous wooden beams supporting the roof.

The railway boom of the mid-1840s, was much urged on by a tycoon of the time, George Hudson, who came from York and built himself a magnificent house in

London. This splendid mansion at 58 Knightsbridge is now the French embassy. It is in stucco, with an impressive staircase and public rooms inside. Hudson crashed; 'a big swollen gambler' Carlyle called him, and with him went the savings of thousands. However, he had one bright idea—that the hundreds of small railway companies should be amalgamated, to prevent duplication and the absurd competition that was growing up. From then on, Parliament gradually assumed regulative control of the railways.

Railway Stations

Another fine monument to the railway's Golden Age is King's Cross. This was built between 1851 and 1852 by the architect and builder Lewis Cubitt (his firm is still putting up buildings in London today). Very plain, just two great arches, it is an engineer's building ornamented only by the central Italianate clock-tower. Inside, there are two glass-vaulted train sheds, which owe a lot to the glass roofing of the Crystal Palace (itself derived from Paxton's Greenhouse). St. Pancras, next door to King's Cross, dates from 1869, and is mentioned later, while Euston has been almost entirely rebuilt. Its buildings were splendidly monumental, with a colossal Doric archway by Philip Hardwick and a Great Hall.

Euston and the Euston Road (which used to be called the New Road) mark the northern limit of London in 1837. At the time of the Railway Mania of the 1840s a Royal Commission on Metropolitan Termini recommended that no new lines should be allowed to penetrate Central London. This made established stations tremendously valuable, since any new lines would have to run into them. London Bridge and Fenchurch Street became more important, particularly for local traffic, and Waterloo was developed as an extension of London Bridge.

Victoria Station, built in 1862 as the terminus for the London, Chatham and Dover Railway.

This decision was also to play a part in the development of the Underground. Paddington was considered far out in the western suburbs, and some connection was needed with the City. We shall see how the first section of the Underground connected Paddington and the other northern termini with Farringdon and the City. The northern stations were particularly involved in such links, since they had a very heavy freight traffic; the southern terminals mostly carried people.

Sanitation

People came, and people stayed. With the coming of the railways, the expansion of London now began in earnest. The overcrowded Georgian slums—'rookeries' as they were called—now had to hold still more people. They came to London with no capital, having to take what work they could, sharing a room, probably a bed, with several others. Servants had to sleep in damp and airless cellars; junior shop assistants slept under the counter. The sanitary conditions were already disgraceful; now they were subjected to such a strain that daily life became a nauseating horror. Through the reports of medical officers and commissioners we learn just what working class life was like. 'I have visited very many places where filth was lying scattered about the rooms, vaults, cellars, areas and yards, so thick, and so deep, that it was hardly possible to move for it. I have also seen in such places human beings living and sleeping in sunk rooms with filth from overflowing cesspools exuding through and running down the walls and over the floors ... the effects of the stench, effluvia and poisonous gases constantly evolving from these foul accumulations were apparent in the haggard, wan and swarthy countenances, and enfeebled limbs, of the poor creatures whom I found residing over and amongst these dens of pollution and wretchedness.'

This was just a small part of the horrifying evidence given to the Metropolitan Sewers Commission in 1847, who also heard that there were thousands of houses in London which had *no drainage whatever*. There were in many places no lavatories, no sewers, no piped water to wash with, or to flush waste away. It is no wonder that the Victorian saying 'Cleanliness is next to Godliness' became so popular when so many were condemned to a hell of dirtiness. Even in 1850, it was estimated that 80,000 houses in London, inhabited by 640,000 people (about one quarter of the total population), were not supplied with piped water.

It was even questionable how lucky were those who did have a water tap. For, unbelievable as it may seem to us, many companies pumped water direct from the 'greatest sewer in London', the Thames, precisely from the points where it was at its foulest. Even now, no fish can live in the river in central London. In the 19th century it often meant drinking death.

A more macabre horror was that overcrowding was not only confined to the living; it also occurred among the dead. According to a report to the government by the great sanitary reformer Edwin Chadwick, 'on spaces of ground which do not exceed 203 acres, closely surrounded by the abodes of the living . . . 20,000 adults and nearly 30,000 youths and children are every year imperfectly interred'. (Note that more young people than adults died.) In Russell Court, off Drury Lane, the whole ground, which had been raised several feet by constant burials, was 'a mass of corruption'. In Rotherhithe, 'interments were so numerous that the half-decomposed organic matter was often thrown up, to make way for fresh graves, exposing sights disgusting, and emitting foul effluvia'.

The burial grounds polluted the air the living had to breathe, and poisoned the well water drunk by those 'unfortunate' enough not to have a piped supply. It was

36

of course mainly the poor who had to live in close proximity to their dead relatives, since they could not afford to bury them at any distance, and so the historic church graveyards and their small additions groaned with overcrowded dead. The middle classes were better off; in the early 1830s cemeteries were laid out to take the remains of those who could pay more. These are well worth a visit, particularly since the more prosperous Victorians were deeply interested in death. This manifested itself in ceremonial death-beds, with the family drawn around and deep mourning. (Whole shops in Oxford Street were devoted to selling black garments for deep mourning and, as grief subsided, they also provided the deep purples and greys which relieved the black.) Gentlemen in mourning wore black armbands, and sometimes black crepe around their tophats. Two of these cemeteries worth visiting are Highgate, which has the Catacombs, a sunken alley of tombs in the Egyptian style, and Kensal Green. Here many people who lived in Tyburnia were buried. The best monuments are in the upper part of the cemetery, huge handsome piles of marble and granite. Look out for the tombs of Morrison, the pill maker, and Ducrow, the circus rider. Brunel is buried here, and so are Thackeray and Trollope.

Besides sanitation, London's workers lacked almost every modern amenity we take for granted. Although the streets, and some houses, had been lit by gas well before Queen Victoria (you can see the cyphers of George IV and William IV still on the classic gas-lamp standards of Regent's Park), in the poorer districts only the streets had light from the blue fish-tail burners (the incandescent mantle came later). Not until the 1890s did piped gas become almost universal, both for cooking and for lighting. In poorer households cooking was done on coal fires, lighting was by candle; and in prosperous homes, by kerosene lamp. The smoke from the coal, plus that from thousands of factory chimneys, from locomotives and

37

stationary steam engines, combined with the damp sea fog which came in from the North Sea and the Channel to produce the Victorian 'pea-souper'.

Public Health

A few men thought that some remedy could be discovered for these ills. Almost alone, they invented the subject of Public Health. One was Edwin Chadwick, the great administrative reformer. When he was dismissed as commissioner of the Board of Health in 1854, *The Times* seemed to think his activities had been an infringement of the liberties of Englishmen (so strong was the spirit of individualism at the time): 'We prefer to take our chance of cholera and the rest, then be bullied into health.' Another of the men who made London healthy to live in was John Simon, first Medical Officer of Health to the City. His reports are not dry-as-dust volumes; they are a passionate plea to the fat aldermen of the City to get down for themselves and see the squalor in which their fellow human beings were condemned to live. Let the educated man, he said, 'devote an hour to visiting some very poor area in the metropolis ... Let him fancy what it would be to himself to live there, in that beastly degradation of stink, fed with such bread, drinking such water ... Let him talk to the inmates, let him hear what is thought of the bone-boiler next door, or the slaughterhouse behind; what of the sewer-grating before the door; what of the Irish basketmakers upstairs—twelve in a room; what of the artisan's dead body, stretched on his widow's one bed, beside her living children.'

Constant disease was the lot of the poor, and as germs are no respecter of class, the rich also suffered. Incredibly, the great cholera epidemic of 1849, when 14,600 people died (over 2000 in one week in September), provoked no remedial action from Parliament. However, the medical men and sanitary reformers pressed forward.

Curious as it may seem to us, they had no idea that the disease was caused by germs. Rather they thought that it, in common with typhoid and other fevers, was caused by an unknown something in the atmosphere, which they called a 'miasma'. However, they did think that dirt and smells encouraged this. They were even able to put their finger on what they called, inside London itself, the 'Capital of Cholera', Jacob's Island, in Bermondsey, commemorated by Jacob Street, near St. Saviour's Dock.

Some street improvements were beginning, but these temporarily made matters worse, as clearing the slums to cut new thoroughfares—like New Oxford Street in 1847 —only pushed people closer together in the remaining rookeries. New Oxford Street made St. Giles and Seven Dials, which were notorious, worse than ever. In these slum areas were also the lodging houses in which lived the immigrants from other parts of England and Ireland who had come to see if the streets of London would really be paved with gold for them. Here is part of a report on such a lodging house in 1850:

'All the beds were occupied, single men being mixed with the couples of the two sexes. The question was never asked, when a man and a woman go to a lodging house, whether they are man and wife. All must pay before they go to bed, or be turned out into the street . . . I have known the bedding to be unchanged for three months . . . They are all infested with vermin, I never met with an exception. No one is required to wash before going to bed in one of these places, unless he has been walking on a wet day without shoes and stockings and then he must bathe his feet.

'The people who slept in the rooms I am describing were chiefly young men, almost all accompanied by young females. I have seen girls of fifteen sleep with "their chaps"—in some places with youths of from sixteen to twenty. There is no objection to any boy or girl occupying a bed, even though the keeper knows that they were previously strangers to each other.

'The accommodation for purposes of decency is very bad in some places. A pail in the middle of the room, to which both sexes may resort, is a frequent arrangement. No delicacy or decency is ever observed.'

The Chartists

A crowded capital filled with ill-used workers is, to anyone with a sense of history, ripe for revolution. In the 1840s England swung from boom to slump and back. There were financial crises, panics and crashes. All were unregulated, however, because the general belief was that to interfere in things would only make them worse. They followed the Malthusian doctrine, that nature supplies its own corrective. Though Marx was unknown in England (the Communist Manifesto dates from 1848) there were home-grown revolutionaries, the Chartists. In April 1848, they decided to act. Demanding what was basically an extension of the franchise (all the six points of the Charter have been met today, except the demand for annual Parliamentary elections) they declared they would march en masse to Parliament to present a monster petition. Seven thousand troops were drafted in, and thousands of middle-class heads of families were sworn in as special constables with white bands on their arms and truncheons as symbols of their authority. Their credibility as a force was not improved by many of them carrying umbrellas.

Troops garrisoned all public buildings, including new ones like the Royal Exchange (1841–44). The Bank of England was surrounded by sand-bags and cannon were positioned on the roof. Gentlemen brought their game-keepers from the country with their guns, and prepared to be besieged. However, the soldiers were largely kept out of sight, and it was the Metropolitan Police who guarded the streets, reinforced by constables who came in from outer areas by train.

A mass meeting was held on Kennington Common, and the Chartists progressed as far as the Thames bridges, but, stopped by the police, they dispersed while the petition went to Parliament in a cab, there to be ridiculed, since some signatures were clumsy or hilarious forgeries.

In the next month the militant Chartists tried again; 80,000 assembled at Clerkenwell and Stepney and afterwards marched through the West End. In August, some of the leaders were arrested. The government alleged that this was just before the flag of revolution was to have been raised in Seven Dials. They were transported, and the Chartist movement disintegrated.

There is no monument to the Chartists on Kennington Common. What does remain is a memento of the Great Exhibition of 1851—Prince Albert's Model Cottages for the Working Classes. Designed by the prince himself, they are practical, and show an ingenious use of the materials available at the time.

London was becoming more cheerful. Its role as a world centre was about to be recognised by the ritual formalities of the world's first international exhibition of art, science and commerce. Prince Albert conceived the first germs of the idea in 1849. The quickening pace of progress was now to find its symbol. The railways now networked England. The country was also joined to the capital by the electric telegraph—used very much in conjunction with the railway. The first line in the world was laid for the Great Western between Paddington and West Drayton in 1838–39. It proved invaluable to the government at the time of the Chartists, and when all the agitation was over, the Electric Telegraph Company presented Whitehall with an extra bill for £500.

Even the lodging houses were tackled in 1851, in time for the Great Exhibition. They were to be registered and inspected by the police, and among the regulations was a provision that any infectious or contagious disease had to be notified. The previous practice had been to pop a new customer into the same bed, and usually the same sheets, as a sick man immediately he had vacated the lodging house.

Entertainment Palaces and Museums

The Crystal Palace

'A little rain fell, just as we started, but before we came near the Crystal Palace the sun shone and gleamed on the gigantic edifice, upon which the flags of all the nations were floating.' So wrote Queen Victoria on May 1, 1851, when she and Albert set out to open 'this Peace-Festival', which united the industry of all the nations of the earth.

Nothing remains today of that glass fantasy built in Hyde Park. It is, however, possible to see where it stood (though curiously no plaque marks the spot) on the long stretch of grass between Rotten Row and the Carriage Road, opposite Rutland Gate. If you go there and look towards the Albert Memorial, you can even see a sickly elm tree, surrounded by railings, on the grass. It may be the last survivor of Colonel Sibthorpe's elm trees. He was the MP who insisted that the trees should not be up-rooted for the exhibition, so Paxton, the gardener who designed the Crystal Palace, revised his design and in-cluded a raised arched transept to include them.

The Crystal Palace was a model of Victorian technology.

The construction of the transept roof of the Crystal Palace. It was specially designed to accommodate a clump of existing elm trees in Hyde Park.

The exterior of the Crystal Palace during the Great Exhibition of 1851; the Exhibition of art, science and commerce was intended to demonstrate the achievements of ordered progress.

It was made out of the most modern materials—or rather, since iron and glass had been known for thousands of years, of materials responding to the most modern treatment. There had never been so much glass used before, and never in such large sheets. The iron used was mostly in the form of tubular iron pillars, which, being hollow, acted also as conduits to take away the water from the roof when it rained. Above all, the Palace was factory-made, prefabricated in standard sections, so that it could be erected in a shorter time than any conventional building; it was almost equally easy to take down, so no trace remains. At the entrance to Kensington Gardens, however, there is a gate which once stood inside the Crystal Palace and the monument outside the Albert Hall was intended to mark the site of the Great Exhibition.

The Crystal Palace fired everybody's imagination. Thousands poured into London from home and abroad. Everyone made money—business people, the government (whose income from licence duty on London road vehicles went up by 30 per cent) and even the Commissioners of the Exhibition, who were able from their profits to begin a scheme for turning a large tract of South Kensington into a cultural quarter. The great museums, the Victoria and Albert, the Science, Natural History and the rest, all stemmed from Albert's successful venture. But what really impressed the public was that optimism had succeeded. All the dire fears—that the congregation of people would lead to revolution, to vice and disorder—proved completely unfounded. The Exhibition, which was essentially educational and serious in its intention, attracted the working class as well as the middle class. It was possible to work for social progress, and people did respond. Afterwards many Victorian amusements became instructional in character.

The Crystal Palace was so popular that a strong feeling developed about its removal. Eventually, a company was formed to re-erect it elsewhere, and a site in south London, at Sydenham, was chosen. An enlarged and more elaborate glass palace went up there, but in 1936 it was utterly destroyed by fire. It is a melancholy experience to wander over the site. Relics of the great terraced gardens, weathered statuary and ornamental urns remain. In the park nearby, however, are some very substantial reminders of the Palace, and in excellent repair. These are the life-size models of prehistoric monsters—the megalosaurus, the ichthyosaurus etc.—all on an island in a lake, sitting amidst the foliage. They once played an instructive role to knicker-bockered Victorian boys and crinolined girls. The Palace was rather similar in its appeal to Madame Tussaud's and Kew Gardens, a sports centre and a popular museum. There were few genuine articles of value from the past; most of the statues were plaster casts.

Daily concerts were given at the Crystal Palace and later gigantic firework displays every Thursday and Saturday evening in summer. The concerts might be in the 4000-seater Concert Hall, or in the 2000-seater Opera House. There was the so-called Great Orchestra, which could also accommodate 4000 people, as well as a 4384 pipe organ worked by hydraulic machinery.

Two stations, the High Level and Low Level, were constructed especially to bring the millions to the Crystal Palace; you could buy a railway ticket which also included admission. The Low Level is still used; the High Level has been demolished. There was even a hotel, the Queen's, Church Road, Upper Norwood, which catered for provincial families who wished to make the Palace the focus of their visit to the metropolis. It still stands, modernised, and catering mostly for businessmen.

Other Public Buildings

The influence of the Crystal Palace was twofold: architectural and cultural. Architecturally, as we have noted

47

with King's Cross station (1851–52), glass on arches had been accepted as the best way of roofing vast spaces. The same contractors who built the Crystal Palace went straight on to build the great covered area of Paddington station. Internally, Paddington is the finest of the great Victorian termini. It is by Brunel and Digby Wyatt, and it really is immense—whole villages could be put inside it. Look up and around, and see the special way in which everything has been designed to fit in with the general scheme, including the decorative metalwork. (The maze of goods buildings nearby, and the great girders of the bridges which cross and recross the line are also worth exploring.)

The contractors were so confident of the speed of prefabrication that they undertook to build the first half of the station in five months. Actually, they took just over a year; but consider that it took 25 years to build the Houses of Parliament, and you will see the contrast.

On a smaller scale, the 'spirit of the Great Exhibition', according to Dr. Pevsner, the great authority on London's buildings, can be experienced in the Floral Hall (1895) in Covent Garden Market. This was once an annexe of the Opera House, but it has been taken over by the fruit and flower people, and you can wander around, admiring the glass and iron of this miniature Crystal Palace.

Factory prefabrication of buildings became quite an industry. Churches, assembly-rooms, houses and warehouses were all preconstructed and often exported to the colonies or America. Structures like clocktowers were also made in the factory, and then simply erected. One example is the Jubilee clocktower in Willesden. A less glamorous but very useful item to be prefabricated was the cast-iron public lavatory. There is a good example in Star Yard, Holborn, elaborately decorated with motifs, including the Royal Arms.

It was of course the railways which carried these

heavy loads of prefabricated materials to their destinations. The railways were also responsible for he changing face of London after 1851. Until that time most houses and buildings had to be made of materials that were near at hand. This was usually bricks, which were easy to transport in small horse-drawn loads. They could even be baked on the spot, if the clay excavated for the foundations was suitable. We have seen that Regency and early Victorian architects, realising that bare brick would be out of scale for their larger buildings resorted to stucco. But now the whole of England, or even Europe, could be a quarry for the building of London. Welsh and Cornish slate for roofs began to arrive, limestone from Devon, sandstone, red, yellow, purple bricks, Cornish granite, and marble from Ireland.

The uniform appearance of London streets began to vanish, and the new buildings stood out in a variety of colours (and styles)—that is, until smoke and grime reduced their façades to some sort of similarity. There were new synthetic materials too—terracotta, maiolica and faience, as well as iron and glass. It is said that the last large public building to be built out of brick alone was the Langham Hotel. This still stands opposite the BBC in Portland Place, and is now BBC offices. Ouida, the Victorian lady novelist who wrote, for her day, scandalous romances, had a suite there. Charing Cross station—that is, the hotel façade—was one of the very first London buildings to use terracotta on a large scale.

These new materials, and factory fabrication, meant that decoration was simplified, and added very little, if anything, to the cost of the final product. So Victorian buildings blossomed out in a riot of colour, curves, embossed decoration and bricks in several hues. To see the results walk along almost any street in the inner suburbs built after 1860—Clapham, say, or Kilburn. The lower windows are usually shallow bays, the tops of which, as well as the door lintels, are ornamented with some cheap cast decoration. There may be a band of ornamental brick or tile on the house too. Along the top of the roof there may be a line of decorative tiles, while on larger houses, there might be quantities of ironwork, particularly if they have a tower feature, which was popular in better class districts like Sydenham or Lewisham.

The public buildings of the time are often coarse and unsubtle in feeling, but they have great contrast, mass and depth created by the projection of ornament on their façades. Many can be found in the City. The Westminster Bank, Lombard Street, is an interesting 'classical' example, while for 'Gothic' try perhaps 33–35 Eastcheap and Mappin & Webb, on the south side of Poultry. Even better are the Gothic façade of St. Pancras Station (at present being used as British Rail offices) and the Foreign Office in Whitehall. These two buildings are both by the same architect, Sir Giles Gilbert Scott. The same architectural feeling, this time based on the style of the French Renaissance, can be found on the north side of Clapham Common where there are two monstrous black terraces, Cedar Terrace and Thornton Terrace (1860), now used as university halls of residence. Look too at the Grosvenor Hotel, built as part of Victoria Station in 1860–61. This was a luxury hotel and the decoration is very lavish. In the spandrels of the arches on the first and top floors are terracotta medallions of contemporary personalities—Victoria, Albert, Palmerston, and so on.

The building of institutions in the spirit of the Crystal Palace now began. The South Kensington cultural site, built with the profits of the Great Exhibition, was pressed into the service of the cause of popular culture. In 1856 buildings in sheet iron and glass were put up in South Kensington, to display some of the objects from the exhibition of 1851 which had either been purchased by the Commissioners or were gifts from their makers. These unusual edifices were nicknamed the 'Brompton

Boilers'. When they were taken down later, they were removed to Bethnal Green, to form part of the roofing of the Museum there.

The Bethnal Green Museum

The Bethnal Green Museum in Cambridge Heath Road, E.2., was opened in 1875, and today is a branch of the Victoria and Albert. It is unrivalled as a place for a quick look at Victoriana. There are statues and other objects which were exhibited in 1851, and a general air of instruction which is typical of the Crystal Palace spirit. It is very near to Victoria Park, which was meant to provide the poor of the East End with open-air, healthy sports, like cricket and gymnastics. Here there is a fine Gothic drinking fountain given by the Baroness Burdett Coutts, of whom we shall hear more in connection with the rehousing of the working classes.

The Victoria and Albert Museum

As the complex of museums and activities in South Kensington took shape they became very popular. (Queen Victoria, as so often, proved to be less 'Victorian' than her subjects, and wanted the museums to open on Sundays. Parliament would not permit this.) The earliest building remaining at South Kensington today are parts of the Victoria and Albert. The façade of the great museum is quite late, designed in 1891 and built ten years later. Within the labyrinthine interior of the museum are large courts on the east side; other ranges of the main courtyard were put up in 1865–66.

In 1867 William Morris decorated the refreshment rooms of the museum. This suite is at the moment used for storage only, but it is hoped to restore these rooms, as they will make a perfect setting for Victorian displays.

The Huxley Building, in Exhibition Road, which adjoins the Victoria and Albert and is part of Imperial

College, was built in 1868. It is very attractive and colourful. Together with the end of the museum it faces the extraordinary Natural History Museum, a Gothic cathedral with a captive congregation of stuffed animals. The architect was Alfred Waterhouse, who put up some of the clumsiest buildings of the time. Other big buildings of his are the Prudential Insurance in High Holborn and University College Hospital, Gower Street. He liked to use terracotta motifs, and if you look up at the Natural History Museum's façade small animals look back at you.

In the South Kensington cultural complex the late Victorians built the Imperial Institute after the great Colonial Exhibition of 1886. It was recently pulled down, but after a great outcry, the tower of the Institute, 280 feet high, was allowed to remain. It, like its lost halls of empire, is by Collcutt. The Institute was yet another place of instruction for Londoners to go on wet afternoons.

It is to the Victorians too that we owe the expansion of the National Gallery and the British Museum. Both of these buildings were substantially complete before 1837, though the Reading Room in the museum, with its great iron dome, was built in 1857. However, the natural history collection occupied much space in the British Museum until it was despatched to Kensington. The Royal Academy was also moved out of the National Gallery to Burlington House, and the space was used for more pictures, particularly Italian primitives. The Tate Gallery was a late Victorian innovation, built in 1897 on the site of the great Millbank Penitentiary, which stands out on maps of before that date as a great geometrically divided circle. It covered 18 acres.

Burlington House, extending from Piccadilly to Burlington Gardens, was the home of the Royal Academy, where it was joined by other learned societies and the University of London (then purely an examining body). While Burlington House looks today all-of-a-piece, a typical Victorian essay in the Italian Renaissance, its core is a much earlier house, covered over by the ornamental pink granite columns and statues of artists and scientists. The exteriors are dated from about 1867.

Alexandra Palace

The most unfortunate imitation of the Crystal Palace was at Muswell Hill, where in the early 70s an attempt was made to provide an equivalent to the complex at Sydenham for North London. This was the Alexandra Palace, named after the beautiful Princess of Wales. It was gutted by fire a few days after it opened, and rebuilt in 1875. It was equipped with one of the largest organs in the world, and the concert hall took 14,000 people. It now is completely empty though sometimes still used for exhibitions; go then and you can stroll through this intensely melancholy structure, filled with courts, halls and passages—a monument to failure.

Another imaginative venture which did not work in North London was the plan to build the greatest of all London's pleasure grounds at Wembley Park. Served by the Metropolitan Railway, the site was intended to include an ironwork tower 1,000 feet high, London's reply to the one built in Paris by Eiffel. It only reached 200 feet, and was eventually demolished in 1907.

All these schemes were vastly influenced by the mobility brought about by the railways. Indeed, the railways often put some money of their own into such entertainments, to generate traffic. Excursions to Windsor, Brighton, and to sporting events like the Cup Final (held at Kennington Oval and then, after 1895, at the Crystal Palace) all became part of the life of the Londoner.

The opening of the Alexandra Palace (1873), an exhibition hall in
north London inspired by the Crystal Palace. It had a disastrous
history, dogged by fire and failure.

Vice and Virtue

The visitor to London in 1851 dipping into *Murray's Handbook for Modern London* could read: 'London should be seen between May and July. Saturday is the aristocratic day for sight-seeing; Monday is generally a workman's holiday. Never listen to those who offer "smuggled" cigars in the street. Beware of mock auctions at shops. Avoid gambling houses or "hells". Gambling is illegal in England, its professors are low rogues and cheating blacklegs. Never dispute in the street with a cabman. If he is insolent and still demands an exorbitant fare, take his number and summons him before the magistrate of the division in which the offence was committed. There are ten deliveries of letters in London daily; and within the circle of three miles from the General Post Office and still within the environs, six daily.'

According to Murray, London was a city of law and order, with an efficient police force and postal system. (Rowland Hill had introduced the penny post in 1840. Previously the recipient paid, and often exorbitantly, according both to the distance travelled and how many sheets there were in the letter.) However, there is also a clear warning against 'low' characters.

Prostitution

The extent of London's Victorian underworld, its beggars, pickpockets and prostitutes, has been recorded for us by Henry Mayhew in his book *London Labour and the London Poor*. He loved to talk to the criminal classes, prostitutes in particular. Mr. Gladstone would also sally out, walking-stick in hand, and chat to girls who were obviously on the streets; his avowed purpose was to 'save' them by persuading them to enter a home for rehabilitation. This was certainly an odd hobby for a Prime Minister during his spare moments in London, and Queen Victoria at one point was quite prepared to believe that his motives were not entirely disinterested. 'Dizzy', who hated Gladstone's hypocrisy, once said that he didn't mind Gladstone having the Ace of Clubs up his sleeve, but what he did object to was Gladstone's assertion that the Holy Ghost had put it there.

It is nevertheless true that in Victorian times London abounded in prostitutes. Being 'gay', the girls called it. They were many thousands—in 1862 an estimate of 80,000 was considered a conservative figure.

London in mid-century, as we have already seen, was a city filled with immigrants, a floating population from Ireland and all the provincial parts of England. There was a huge population of servant-girls and an equal number of young unmarried men of the working and lower middle class. We must also remember that London was the principal manufacturing centre of the kingdom, and much of the work was done in small and sordid sweat-shops.

The employers of servant-girls rather expected them to have a 'follower', a young man who would often be seen

56

'A disgraceful scene at a fancy house (1864)', where young men about town could meet women of dubious reputation. Prostitution was rife in Victorian times.

hanging around outside the servants' entrance. And no matter how proper a household was, a good servant, providing she was discreet, undoubtedly had her love affairs tolerated. The story of the housemaid who asked her mistress if she could keep her baby with the remark, 'It's only a little one, ma'am', has the ring of a story often paralleled in real life. Often such girls and their suitors could not really contemplate marriage, so they did the best they could. Victorian illegitimacy figures were high.

In some households, wages were so pitifully small for the lower maids that some of them became amateur prostitutes; the demand was great for such services and the only way to earn a little extra was on the streets.

Life was also restricted for the men of middle class, as far as meeting girls of their own station was concerned; these were usually closely guarded and chaperoned until marriage. So the men turned to prostitutes—a habit, in the form of a kept mistress, that often continued after marriage. Victorian soldiers and sailors too were discouraged from marrying, and were always out looking for pick-ups in the parks.

The areas most frequented by prostitutes were the whole extent of Regent Street, from its beginning in Waterloo Place to Portland Place, and the Bayswater Road. Tottenham Court Road and the Waterloo Road were also regular 'beats'. In Stepney, where the women were of the lowest, catering for sailors and petty tradesmen, arrests were highest. Cremorne Gardens in summer was popular as a meeting place with well-off men.

A full description of London's underworld of the time can be got from Mayhew's book, along with a long account of slang terms and the odd names of some of the characters; 'Swindling Sall' and 'Lushing Loo' are mild examples.

The criminal class Mayhew depicts must be seen against the background of the slum horrors described in Chapter 3. Working conditions were equally bad, and there was no system of social security to look after people if they were ill; just primitive hospitals if they were lucky, and such charity as they could get. Born in the slums, without hope of improving themselves and, in a time when depressions and a consequent immediate paying off of workers were frequent, the poor often had to steal or starve.

A girl with a pretty face could, if she came from Stepney or Seven Dials, count herself lucky if her looks attracted a rich admirer. Not all Victorian 'fallen women' were street-walkers. Quite a large number had permanent relations with the rich and powerful, who set them up in villas in St. John's Wood or some other pleasant neighbourhood. Often the protector would see that they were educated, and one such apt pupil wrote to *The Times* in 1858 on the realities of a working woman's existence:

'As for their virtue, they lose it as one loses his watch who is robbed by the highway thief. Their virtue is the watch and society is the thief. These poor women toiling on starvation wages, while penury, misery, and famine clutch them by the throat and say "Render up your body or die".'

Then she digs her knife deep into hypocrisy: 'Admire this magnificent shop in this fashionable street; its front, fittings and decorations cost no less than a thousand pounds. The respectable master of the establishment keeps his carriage and lives in his country house. He has daughters too; his patronesses are fine ladies ... Do they think, as they admire the taste and elegance of that tradesman's show, of the poor creatures who wrought it, and what they are paid for it. Do they reflect on the weary toiling fingers, on the eyes dim with watching, on the bowels yearning with hunger, on the bended frames, on the broken constitutions, on poor human nature driven to its coldest corner and reduced to its narrowest means in the production of these ornaments?'

Girls in the sewing rooms behind such Oxford Street shops as Marshall & Snelgrove would sew between 8.30 am and 7 pm, and later during the season. Conditions were similar for girls at Swan and Edgar, or at Jay's Mourning establishment at Oxford Circus. During the season sewing all night for ball dresses was common. An order would be given at four in the afternoon for an elaborate ball dress to be made and delivered before 12 the same night. Worse conditions could be found in the factories. In particular, we read of the horrors of some of the match-making factories, where the phosphorus used in the heads would poison the workers, resulting in 'phossy jaw', causing the teeth and even jaw to drop off.

Patent Medicines

Medical facilities were so inadequate and so expensive that most working-class people resorted to patent medicines, which usually promised much, but usually contained little more than aloes and powdered ginger. They made the fortunes of their manufacturers. Thomas Holloway was the greatest maker of pills in London. He made a huge fortune of over five million pounds, speculating successfully and becoming in every way a model capitalist. With some of his money he built the Royal Holloway College, which can be seen in all its grandeur at Egham. It is a free copy in stone and red brick of the Château de Chambord and houses a splendid collection of Victorian painting. Holloway also put up the money for a sanatorium at Virginia Water 'for the treatment of mental illness among the less prosperous middle classes'.

Such preparations, if taken for serious illnesses, were worse than useless, since they delayed real medical help. This was particularly true of venereal diseases, far more common in Victorian times than today and from which no complete recovery was possible in advanced cases. There were all kinds of thinly disguised advertisements for

An operation in the early days of antiseptic surgery. The antiseptic spray, invented by Lister, was first used in 1865.

'cures' to these diseases. Other advertisements hinted that the pills offered could procure abortions (of which there were a very great number in Victorian times). Contraception was known and seems to have been practised increasingly from the 1870s.

Most prisons until the 1870s dated from the previous era. Newgate was still in use, as were Horsemonger Gaol and the Millbank Penitentiary. But by the end of the century Holloway, Wandsworth and Pentonville had been added to their number.

Prisoners were made to work a treadmill or pick oakum. Until 1868 executions took place in public. Charles Dickens gave an account of one in 1849:

'I believe that a sight so inconceivably awful as the wickedness and levity of the immense crowd collected at that execution could be imagined by no man . . . When the two miserable creatures who attracted all this ghastly sight about them were turned quivering in the air . . . there was no more thought that two immortal souls had gone to judgement, no more restraint of the previous obscenities than if the name of Christ had never been heard in this world. . . .'

In many aspects, mid-Victorian society was so brutal that we can understand the strength of the reaction, particularly the religious reaction, against these conditions. Societies flooded London with religious tracts—although many of the poor could not read. There were missions, such as the London City Mission, established in 1835, and the Open-Air Mission (1853). They went through London talking of sin and salvation. There were other foundations, including the YMCA founded in 1844 and the Temperance Societies, to which can be added the Metropolitan Free Drinking Fountain Association, which aimed to provide a free and refreshing drink of water and so give an alternative to the public house to the thirsty. Many of these fountains still survive (as do drinking troughs for animals; there is a fine one in Wellington

Road, St. John's Wood, and another at Islington Green).

The Salvation Army started its work in the East End in 1865, when William Booth held his first Army meeting outside the Blind Beggar public house in the Mile End Road. The 'Sally' Army built citadels all over London. As it is the most typical religious movement to be formed in Victorian times, these buildings are worth going to see; examples can be found at Wood Green, Lewisham and Harlesden.

During the period there was a boom in the building of churches and chapels of all kinds. Interest in religion became intense, and crowds would flock to the great preachers of the period, like Spurgeon, whose vast tabernacle was at the Elephant and Castle. There are so many Victorian churches—which by 1840 were almost universally in the Gothic style—that it is difficult to compile a list. (From the 1880s some Roman Catholic buildings were in Baroque style, like Brompton Oratory, or Byzantine, like Westminster Cathedral.) They are set out in Dr. Pevsner's two volumes on *The Buildings of London*, St. Augustine's, Kilburn, however, is a particularly splendid example.

But despite the number of churches, it would seem that a great many people, particularly of the poorer classes, never went near a church, so the impression that it was a time of universal church-going is misleading.

Theatres and Diversions

The Victorian middle-classes thought the theatre was only one step removed from the brothel. The theatre in London had declined completely from its 18th-century position of triumph. Larger theatres had meant an abandonment of subtlety, and melodrama—gross exaggeration in acting and in plot—was already established by the time Victoria became queen. As a result, the class of persons who made up the audience declined, and so the British stage was caught in a vicious circle. By 1851, only two theatres were patronised by the aristocracy and the respectable, Her Majesty's in the Haymarket, where Italian opera was performed, and The Royal Italian Opera House, Covent Garden, today's Royal Opera House. In both theatres admission was only granted to those in evening dress, thus ensuring that the riff-raff were kept out. Today's Covent Garden dates from 1858, a fine interior with a relief of the queen's profile, in her prime, above the stage. The modern Haymarket is the late Victorian theatre of 1897.

The queen loved the opera, and often went there.

Above: *The entrance to Victoria Dwellings, Clerkenwell Road, one of many 'model' buildings put up to house the working class.*

Right: *A horse bus in 1868. The first horse-drawn buses began in 1829 and continued until the present century.*

Previous page: *One of the many statues of Queen Victoria, here on the south-facing panel of Temple Bar in Fleet Street.*

LONDON BRIDGE RYS
RED LION
WALHAM
GREEN
BANK
FULHAM
HYDE
PARK
CORNER
SLOANE ST PICCADILLY, CHARING + STRAND.
PUTNEY

Top: *A contemporary photograph (1862) of the sewer below Abbey Mills pumping station, built as part of Joseph Bazalgette's new drainage system for London.*

Above: *The launching of the* Great Eastern *at Millwall in 1857; built by Brunel, it was one of the first 'iron' ships. Later, London declined as a ship-building centre.*

Right: *A personification of agriculture on the Holborn Viaduct.*

Above: *Smith's umbrella shop in Holborn, which still retains its Victorian shop front.*

Right: *Part of the Albert Memorial (1863–72), designed by Sir Giles Gilbert Scott. Large, lavish and ornate, it epitomises High Victorian taste.*

Next page: *Smithfield Meat Market, an ironwork structure built in 1868 to handle both home-killed and imported carcases.*

Audiences at the ordinary theatres were too rough for the queen to venture into, so command performances were arranged for the court at Buckingham Palace, Windsor, and even Balmoral. (There were none for 20 years after Prince Albert's death.) The queen saw the Gilbert and Sullivan operas in this way.

A look at the London theatres in 1851 shows the complete eclipse of all serious drama. The taste was for melodrama, spectacle, farce and burlesque. Two theatres were devoted to horsemanship mixed with melodrama. The most famous was Astley's, of which Ducrow had been a famous star. Most of the theatres have disappeared but the only substantial one of that time in South London, the Victoria in the Waterloo Road, is now the Old Vic. It is comparatively unchanged, and brings home the size of a popular house of the time. Augustus Sala, visiting the 'Vic' in 1859, describes the 'coarse deal benches in the coarsely and tawdrily-decorated cheap theatre', but he points out that in the dramas of the time, for all their silliness, 'immutable principles of right and justice are asserted'. He thought that it was better for the audience to pay their threepence to sit in the gallery of the 'Vic' and get some moral education, however clumsy, than 'gamble in low coffee shops, break each other's heads in public houses, . . . or lie in wait in doorways to rob and murder'.

Theatrical programmes were very long and often included several short plays; often a comedy would be mixed with a horror melodrama. The music-hall, that Victorian theatrical experience which is today considered so typical of the time, developed from singing rooms in public houses, and so the audience singing and joining in the chorus immediately becomes understandable, as does the idea of a master of ceremonies. The first music-hall was Canterbury Hall, off Westminster Road, which opened in 1849. In the 1860s there were 23 in London, of which one, on the site of the Oxford Street Corner

House, had 428,000 customers a year. Many of the earlier music-halls, like the theatres, were very open to fire risk, and often burnt down. Of those that survive, the Camden is now a BBC television theatre, and another, the famous Collins's, facing Islington Green, closed recently; only the façade now remains. Others that linger on as theatres or cinemas include the London Pavilion in Piccadilly Circus and the Hippodrome in St. Martin's Lane.

With the rise of Henry Irving and T. W. Robertson the Victorian theatre established its merit in the eyes of the middle classes. Robertson, a dramatist, worked with Sir George and Lady Bancroft, both actors, to produce a new, natural theatre, where people did the things they usually do in real life, and where the sets were similar to the surroundings of ordinary middle-class or upper-class people. The new departure drew a middle-class audience to the theatre, as well as getting upper-class patrons of the opera to take an interest in straight plays again. No longer, too, were there 'curtain raisers', or other short pieces, but only one play on the evening's bill. Their first success was *Society* (1865), a satire on the materialism of the age.

Sir Henry Irving, the first actor to be knighted, typifies the acceptance of his profession by the Victorian establishment. He had started in superior melodrama, his first success being *The Bells* (1871). Sensing his own limitations as an actor, he surrounded himself with a superb company, who complemented his own performance. His company made its home in the Lyceum Theatre in Wellington Street, off the Strand. This is one of the older theatres of London, dating from 1809, and is now a dance hall. Irving reigned at the Lyceum between 1879–1903.

The most living part of the Victorian theatre was of course Gilbert and Sullivan. Even now there is a London season every year devoted to their works by their own D'Oyly Carte company. The words should be carefully

listened to for a picture of London life at the time they were written (1875–89). Nothing can better illustrate the way in which the theatre had become accepted by the middle classes than these works, performed all over the English-speaking world, and particularly popular with school and amateur groups. There is nothing, as Gilbert once rightly claimed, in the operas to offend even the most delicately brought-up lady; they made the fortunes of their creators and that of their impresario, Richard D'Oyly Carte. With the money he made he built the Palace Theatre in Shaftesbury Avenue. It was to be a theatre for the performance of Sullivan's grand opera *Ivanhoe* (1891), which was a failure. The theatre is splendidly ornate, the exterior a maze of terracotta decoration, while inside there is a rich display of coloured marble. D'Oyly Carte also built the Savoy Hotel, where many of the suites are named after the Gilbert and Sullivan operas.

Other places of Victorian amusement were the moving panoramas and dioramas. These were in some way the forerunners of the cinema, in that no live performers were used. Many are listed in 1851: the Cyclorama (the earthquake in Lisbon in 1755); the Diorama, Regent's Park, which still survives at 9–10 Park Square East ('Etna in Sicily under three effects, evening, sunrise and an eruption'); the Panorama ('moving pictures of the Bosphorus, the Dardanelles, and Constantinople'), to name just a few. Another sight was 'The Incubator, or Egg-hatching Machine, Leicester Square—the whole process of hatching by artificial heat is here exhibited. Admission 1s.'. And then, of course, there was Madame Tussaud's and the old amusement gardens at Cremorne, Chelsea and Vauxhall.

By the 1870s there were also the permanent halls and galleries in South Kensington for annual exhibitions, and the Royal Albert Hall. Capable of holding 10,000 people, it was designed for musical entertainments, concerts, exhibitions, public meetings and balls. It has two concentric walls, between which are the staircases and corridors, and a glass dome supported by iron ribs. Opened in 1871, it has since played a huge part, particularly with the Promenade Concerts in our own day, in the musical life of London. The Victorians loved Handel, and his works were performed both at the Albert Hall and the Crystal Palace.

Metropolitan Improvements

For most of the 19th century, London was ▮ government of its own. The other big cities of ▮ received powers of local government in 1835. T▮ polis did not. This was mainly due to the vest▮ of the City Corporation, which still remained ▮ (and whose constitution to this day is largely ▮ And while the conditions of the poor in ▮ manufacturing cities were no better than in ▮ very size of London and the lack of any cent▮ undoubtedly made things worse. The City ▮ itself. The rest of the metropolis was go▮ number of bodies in each locality, some sp▮ for a particular purpose.

There were local parish vestries, th▮ Guardians, the Commissioners of Sewers, ▮ one had overall authority; there was no ▮ persons on which to lay the blame. The ri▮ merchants of the City constantly worked ▮ control of the immense riches of their a▮ their own hands, to be used to their ▮

listened to for a picture of London life at the time they were written (1875–89). Nothing can better illustrate the way in which the theatre had become accepted by the middle classes than these works, performed all over the English-speaking world, and particularly popular with school and amateur groups. There is nothing, as Gilbert once rightly claimed, in the operas to offend even the most delicately brought-up lady; they made the fortunes of their creators and that of their impresario, Richard D'Oyly Carte. With the money he made he built the Palace Theatre in Shaftesbury Avenue. It was to be a theatre for the performance of Sullivan's grand opera *Ivanhoe* (1891), which was a failure. The theatre is splendidly ornate, the exterior a maze of terracotta decoration, while inside there is a rich display of coloured marble. D'Oyly Carte also built the Savoy Hotel, where many of the suites are named after the Gilbert and Sullivan operas.

Other places of Victorian amusement were the moving panoramas and dioramas. These were in some way the forerunners of the cinema, in that no live performers were used. Many are listed in 1851: the Cyclorama (the earthquake in Lisbon in 1755); the Diorama, Regent's Park, which still survives at 9–10 Park Square East ('Etna in Sicily under three effects, evening, sunrise and an eruption'); the Panorama ('moving pictures of the Bosphorus, the Dardanelles, and Constantinople'), to name just a few. Another sight was 'The Incubator, or Egg-hatching Machine, Leicester Square—the whole process of hatching by artificial heat is here exhibited. Admission 1s.'. And then, of course, there was Madame Tussaud's and the old amusement gardens at Cremorne, Chelsea and Vauxhall.

By the 1870s there were also the permanent halls and galleries in South Kensington for annual exhibitions, and the Royal Albert Hall. Capable of holding 10,000 people, it was designed for musical entertainments, concerts, exhibitions, public meetings and balls. It has two concentric walls, between which are the staircases and corridors, and a glass dome supported by iron ribs. Opened in 1871, it has since played a huge part, particularly with the Promenade Concerts in our own day, in the musical life of London. The Victorians loved Handel, and his works were performed both at the Albert Hall and the Crystal Palace.

Metropolitan Improvements

For most of the 19th century, London was without a government of its own. The other big cities of England received powers of local government in 1835. The metropolis did not. This was mainly due to the vested interest of the City Corporation, which still remained unreformed (and whose constitution to this day is largely medieval). And while the conditions of the poor in other great manufacturing cities were no better than in London, the very size of London and the lack of any central authority undoubtedly made things worse. The City looked after itself. The rest of the metropolis was governed by a number of bodies in each locality, some specially set up for a particular purpose.

There were local parish vestries, the Poor Law Guardians, the Commissioners of Sewers, and so on. No one had overall authority; there was no one group of persons on which to lay the blame. The rich bankers and merchants of the City constantly worked to ensure that control of the immense riches of their area remained in their own hands, to be used to their own advantage,

Holborn Viaduct, opened in 1869 to carry traffic between Holborn and the City across Farringdon Street.

and that Bills in Parliament which threatened their own privileged position were defeated.

However, it became apparent even to the most reactionary City magnates that the only way to improve the sanitary plight of London was to co-operate with the other authorities to stem the tide of sewage and disease. In 1855 Sir Benjamin Hall (after whom 'Big Ben' is named) introduced an Act 'for the Better Local Management of the Metropolis'. The 300 tiny local bodies were swept away, and 38 districts were formed by regrouping many of the old parishes. These districts became the local authorities responsible for such matters as public health, highways and lighting.

But the most important part of the Act was to create a central authority for all London, the Metropolitan Board of Works. Under this unromantically named body, the chaos which was London was transformed. For, while the main purpose in creating the Board was to take the sewers out of the hands of the inefficient Commissioners who had hitherto run them, as time went on the Board acquired new powers, partly special to London, such as the embanking of the Thames, but also as the local authority administering the new Acts that Parliament began to pass for the welfare of all parts of the country. The Board came to control the regulations governing explosives, gas and petrol, weights and measures, and so on. The Board was indirectly elected by all the local authorities of London, including the City.

London's sewers

For the sewers, they found an engineer of genius in Joseph Bazalgette. He planned a new system of main drainage for the entire city, which was begun in 1859. The object was to change the role of the Thames from that of principal sewer—that is, to divert the waste matter and carry it away to be discharged where tidal currents could not wash it back.

71

A series of large sewers, which were in fact tunnels, was constructed on both sides of the Thames to a total length of 85 miles. They intercepted the old sewers at right angles, and were designed to discharge their contents at Barking Creek on the north bank, and at Crossness, near Plumstead, on the south. Because Bazalgette's sewers were below the levels of existing ones, gravitation and rainfall cleared most of the waste away. But where the land level was low, pumping by steam-engines was necessary and four great pumping stations were constructed. They are at Abbey Mills (Stratford), Pimlico, Deptford and Crossness. All remain, except for Crossness, which has been rebuilt. The sewage was also, during the pumping process,'de-odourised'. The Prince of Wales opened Crossness in 1864, a sign of the importance given to the project.

The most splendid of the remaining three stations is Abbey Mills. The buildings are magnificent, in Gothic-Byzantine style. The ironwork inside is complex and yet somehow utilitarian, in spite of the decorative swirls. It was originally worked by great beam engines—some of which still function today, for example, at the Ram Brewery in Wandsworth.

As the Board's engineer, Bazalgette was also involved in their programme of metropolitan improvements. This involved cutting new streets and improving old ones, and building the Victoria, Albert and Chelsea Embankments. Appropriately, his statue stands today on the Victoria Embankment, near Hungerford bridge.

The Underground Railways

The Victoria Embankment was not only 30 acres regained from the Thames, it was also a site for underground work. Two great tunnels were made underneath it, the upper containing water pipes, gas pipes and telegraph wires, the lower another of Bazalgette's great sewers. It is indeed to the Metropolitan Board of Works that we owe so much of that vital part of today's subterranean London. Whenever the Board put in a new street, they were also very careful to create great vaults and tunnels underneath it. Yet more tunnels were built alongside those built by Bazalgette. These were to carry the Metropolitan District Railway. The Underground had arrived.

It was on January 10, 1863 that the world's first underground railway went into operation. This, the Metropolitan, ran from Paddington to Farringdon Street. The idea took a long time to realise; a London solicitor of radical mind, Charles Pearson, had been a strong advocate of such a railway since the 1840s. At that time Brunel was experimenting with what was called 'atmospheric traction'. The carriages were to be literally sucked along by creating a vacuum in a tube running between the rails. Inside the tube was a piston connected to the train, and there were stationary engines at intervals along the line to exhaust the air. One of these railways was introduced in the 1840s between Forest Hill and West Croydon. In 1845 the trains achieved 70 mph, but there were tremendous transmission difficulties, and the railway was dismantled. One of the engine houses, however, still stands, at Croydon Water Department, 43 Wellesley Road, Croydon.

With no magical atmospheric traction, the Underground would have to rely on steam. In 1851 the new terminus at King's Cross was being got ready, and today's Paddington was being constructed. Pearson pressed his idea, and an Act of Parliament giving permission was finally passed in 1853. A great trench was dug, for this was a 'cut-and-cover' construction close to the surface, very different from the deep tubes, which came later. The trench was wide, for it was to take not only the standard tracks but also the Great Western's seven-foot-wide gauge.

A forerunner of the 'tube', worked by suction, at the Crystal Palace in 1864. The first deep underground railway was not opened until 1890.

One passenger in 1863 recorded that there was no 'disagreeable odour' in the underground. The trains condensed their steam. The carriages were lit by gas, carried in iron bottles, which were replenished at intervals. Such stations as Baker Street (Metropolitan Line) and Great Portland Street give quite a good idea of what a Victorian Underground station looked like.

Meanwhile, the South Eastern railway had built its own West End terminus at Charing Cross. The station was opened on January 11, 1864. The hotel, which is an internal part of the station, is very well worth a visit. The dining-room is a superb example of a ceremonial room of this time, and is still kept in splendid state. The lounge, where tea is served (also on the first floor), has a small conservatory, 'Crystal Palace' type extension, and this is also worth looking at, to sample mid-Victorian elegance at its best. The architect was E. M. Barry.

All was now set for an 'inner circle' of Underground lines linking the main termini. Parliament, in a Committee report, came out in favour and the scheme went ahead. The whole embankment project, on the other hand, lagged behind when the Railway Company found it difficult to raise enough capital, and it was the Metropolitan Board of Works which continually urged that the work be hurried along. Finally, the whole Embankment and the railway section was opened on July 13, 1870. The Albert Embankment, opposite the Houses of Parliament on the south side of the river, was opened in 1869, taking only three years to build; the Chelsea Embankment was opened in 1874.

Other Improvements

The three Embankments gave new thoroughfares to London, as well as river promenades. They are all very much as built, with splendid iron lamposts—originally

A suicide at Edgware Road Station on the Metropolitan Line. The Metropolitan, the world's first underground railway, opened in 1863 and ran from Paddington to Farringdon Street.

for gas. Special seats, with the cast-iron ends in the shape of a sphinx, can be seen on the Victoria Embankment.

They were the first great showpieces of the Board in its programme of metropolitan improvements, the construction of new, broader streets both for easing traffic and for providing sites for fine new buildings, usually in areas which were either slummy or somewhat rundown. Their very first new street was Garrick Street, Covent Garden, opened in 1861. This created the precedent for their other streets, with an arched subway under the road to contain all the services and arched side passages to the houses.

In the City, Queen Victoria Street was carved out to provide an eastern extension to the Victoria Embankment route, linking the Houses of Parliament to the Mansion House. There was now a wide clearway free of steep gradients between the two, a new imperial route.

A better connection was now needed between Trafalgar Square and the Victoria Embankment, and the present Northumberland Avenue was built and opened in 1876. To open up this road Northumberland House, the last of the great town houses of the aristocracy in the Strand, had to be pulled down. In 1866, when the Board had attempted to get Parliamentary permission for the new road, the then duke had objected, but his successor was persuaded, sweetened with half-a-million pounds.

Northumberland Avenue should be visited as it provides us with perhaps the best group of Victorian buildings of the late 1870s and early 1880s in central London, not so much from the point of view of artistic merit, but simply for the feeling of the period. The Avenue itself, presumably because of its central position and now excellent communications, became the site for giant hotels. All these have since become offices.

Walking down the Avenue with your back to Trafalgar Square, it is the right-hand side which is completely untouched. Look at Grand Buildings, which are on both sides of the street facing Trafalgar Square; these were both originally the Grand Hotel (built 1878–82). Then on the right you come to the vast Northumberland House, now a War Office warren, but then the Victoria Hotel. The building which is now Nigeria House, where Great Scotland Yard comes into the Avenue, was once the Society for Promoting Christian Knowledge. Charles Waterhouse may have had a hand in designing it. Then comes Metropole Buildings, the former Hotel Metropole. The Metropole (550 bedrooms), the Victoria (500), and the Grand (400) all belonged to the same company and were among the best hotels in London. Prices were: 5s. per night; breakfast, 3s. 6d; lunch, 3s. 6d; dinner, between 5s. and 6s.

Nearby, facing the Embankment, but also fronting Whitehall Place is Whitehall Court, a block of flats of 1884. When seen from the lake in St. James's Park, its splendidly ornate pavilion roofs combine with the Horse Guards, to make the most attractive vista in London. Part of Whitehall Court (where Bernard Shaw once lived) is the National Liberal Club. This is by Waterhouse, and the interior rooms are vast, and decorated with glazed tiles. There are over 80 pictures and busts of Mr. Gladstone in the Club's possession.

The Metropolitan Board of Works also turned its attention to improving north-south communication. Travelling from Euston or King's Cross to the southern stations meant negotiating a maze of mean and narrow streets—only John Nash's Regent Street provided a good route, and that was too far west. 'Most of the narrow and tortuous roads by which traffic was compelled to find its way from Oxford Street to Charing Cross were, during a considerable portion of the day, so occupied with vehicles engaged in transporting merchandise as to be entirely blocked against the ordinary carriage traffic.' Because of this congestion, a new road was cut running from Tottenham Court Road to Trafalgar Square, and called the Charing Cross Road. This was opened in 1887, and intersected Shaftesbury Avenue, another new street cut by the Board, at the new Cambridge Circus. Shaftesbury Avenue was opened in 1886, but it took eight years to complete, because it cut through much of what remained of the St. Giles 'Rookery', and the Board was not allowed to demolish more than 15 houses occupied by working-class families until alternative accommodation was found for them. The Board therefore built ranges of flats—drab barracks, but at least sanitary—near Newport Market, and lined the Charing Cross Road at that point with others (this is south of Cambridge Circus). Parliament finally let the Board off with providing local housing for only a proportion of the people displaced. (The idea was that they worked locally, often in trades which demanded that they rose early or went to bed late, so to remove them to another part of the city would cause great hardship.)

The other improvement, New Oxford Street, which was carried out before the Board's formation in the 1840s, also led to the building of new dwellings for the working classes. They can be seen in Streatham Street, W.C.1., and date from about 1848; they make quite an interesting study in comparative housing.

Shaftesbury Avenue connected Piccadilly to Bloomsbury. Piccadilly Circus was called Regent Circus at that time. It had to wait for its new name until 1893, when the new London County Council also extended the circus so that it became an irregular open space. (Incidentally, far from being Eros, the god of love, the figure on the fountain was intended by the LCC to be 'illustrative of Christian charity'; it is also of aluminium, which was a new and rather expensive material.) There are fine examples of Victorian buildings in Piccadilly Circus: look at the Criterion (1870–85) and the London Pavilion (1885), mentioned earlier.

The Metropolitan Board of Works did not confine itself to central areas; it built Burdett Road in Hackney

An experimental electric tramcar in 1883. These and petrol-driven buses gradually superseded horse-drawn public transport from 1900.

as an approach to Victoria Park, widened Kensington High Street, the Commercial Road in Whitechapel, and improved the Angel, Jamaica Road, Kentish Town Road, to name only a few.

Public Transport

All this road work was badly needed, for the extension of the railways and the speeding up of commerce generally led to the generation of still more street traffic. The steamboat firms on the Thames suffered; in an attempt to maintain services they amalgamated in 1876 to form the London Steamboat Company, but traffic became more and more seasonal. In 1886, when 57 paddle-wheelers were put up for auction, the regular services came to an end; sadly, the boats were unsold.

Omnibuses continued to do quite well. In 1875 the biggest company, the London General, carried nearly 50 million passengers. Tolls on bridges and some stretches of road were removed in the 1860s, and the government's mileage tax on public vehicles was abolished in 1870. There were many small independent bus lines, all with their differently coloured buses. These were plastered with advertisements, so the general effect was lively. In 1881 the London General was faced with a competitor, the London Road Car Company, which introduced a new and better designed bus. The Road Car Company's buses flew small Union Jacks (a hit at the L.G.O. Co., which had been started by Frenchmen, who still held considerable stock). The company also introduced tickets and the bell punch. By 1890, the Road Car Co. had attracted over a quarter of the London General's total number of passengers. Its direct competition on the same routes as its rival led to reduced fares and improvements in vehicles and service.

Another innovation was the tram. These were first drawn by horses, which could carry far more people along a tracked path than they could in an ordinary road vehicle. The trams came in 1870, and brought passengers from the suburbs—Brixton, Camberwell, New Cross, Deptford, Archway, Finsbury Park, Stoke Newington, Stratford—to the centre. However, they were not permitted into the central streets themselves, and did not penetrate beyond the Inner Circle. An extension to Holborn was however allowed in 1885-87, and a connection from Holborn to King's Cross in 1889.

There were now more bridges over the Thames—at Lambeth in 1862, at Battersea in 1858, at Blackfriars in 1869, and at Westminster in 1862, as well as the railway bridges at Battersea for Victoria, at Charing Cross, at Cannon Street and the 'hideous' Alexandra Lattice Bridge, which carried the London Chatham and Dover Railway to Ludgate Hill station. Further upstream there were also new bridges like that at Putney. Look at the splendidly ornate lamps at intervals along the bridge.

The shape of the London we know today had almost arrived.

Suburbia

London in the 19th century became more than a central city; it was now also a city of great sprawling suburbs. This was ensured by the amazing fecundity of the Victorians and their tendency to flock to London. Every year, in the last part of Victoria's reign, London's population grew by 100,000. By 1901, when the queen died, one-sixth of the total population of the kingdom was concentrated in the capital. We have seen in the last chapter how the accommodation in the centre of London became limited as streets were broadened and hotels and offices were put up in the place of slum and other housing. And, as general economic conditions improved—as they did—families demanded more than just a share of a room in a overcrowded slum.

The growth of suburbs provided the answer. Between 1839 and 1850 it was the turn of Tyburnia, spreading over North Kensington, Notting Hill, and Paddington. At the same time Belgravia was created, spreading in the 1850s to Chelsea, Pimlico and Victoria. The houses that the fashionable vacated as they moved west were quickly filled up, but even so there was not enough room. Islington filled up with the middle classes (its population tripled between 1841 and 1861). The East End became more and more crowded—Bethnal Green now replaced Seven Dials as a by-word for slums. Like Whitechapel and Shoreditch, it was without any open space, except for a few churchyards and old burial grounds. Over 600,000 people crammed into these airless areas around 1890. Hackney jumped from 38,000 people in 1861 to 125,000 in 1871, and 199,000 in 1891.

In the 1860s the southern bank of the Thames began to come into its own. As we have just noted the Thames bridges were increasing rapidly in number by that time, and in the 1860s there was an appreciable boom in suburban railway building. Most of these lines were built to the south. The crowded riverside slums of Southwark, which included the notorious Bermondsey, and of Lambeth—where before Bazalgette many of the main sewers were actually open ditches—now had a developing hinterland, which rapidly sent out ribbons of suburban housing along the roads that led to such rural retreats as Streatham, Brixton, Peckham and the rather classy residential village of Clapham.

The areas between the main roads into London now began to be filled in by rows and rows of semi-detached houses—or by monotonous terraces—usually built by speculative builders. Finally, from the 1890s onwards, there was another migration, out to the limits of greater London and beyond, as public transport, particularly the Metropolitan railway's extension to the north-west, made it possible to live many miles away, and yet commute directly and reasonably effortlessly into the City every morning.

Visit to the Suburbs

The only way really to get the atmosphere of these

suburbs is to visit them. There are few buildings of note; there is no artistic statement such as we find in the churches and the public buildings of central London which can, if successful, convey the spirit of the age that built them. The suburbs are the creation and the habitats of hundreds and thousands of little men and women, who did not think of making a monument to their life and time, who went about their daily life more or less in a state of unconscious acceptance.

It is only when we are in them, walking past the rows and rows of semis, seeing the little shops—which, in areas which have 'gone down', will sometimes still have their Victorian shop-fronts—and perhaps one of those enamel advertisements for cocoa or for 'Virol'—that the picture of their life emerges.

Camberwell

The suburb which grew fastest in the second phase of London's expansion, and which filled up the gaps between the main roads into the city, was undoubtedly Camberwell. During Victoria's reign, its population expanded over seven times. It was the suburb for the respectable but not very well off; it contained more clerks than any other part of London.

As time went by the area changed its character; the rule that the better-off withdrew further from London's centre applied. The fine houses of the 1840s on Champion Hill and in the upper part of The Grove were followed by less pleasing designs. Trafalgar Avenue is debased classical, built in 1852. Vicarage Grove, dating from 1866–68, introduced the bay window—a shape which became as universal a feature in Victorian houses as the classic twelve-paned window had been in the previous century. Avondale Square (1875) and Sandover Road (1882) brought elevations which were so hideous that one wonders what on earth was in the mind of the man who 'created' them.

The suburb of Camberwell has been extensively studied by the economic historian Dr H. J. Dyos. His description of these houses of the period from 1871 to the 90s shows a scheme which was typical of many other suburbs besides Camberwell. It is an example of tracts of housing—surely well over a million—which we are still stuck with today.

According to Dyos, the two-storey brick terrace was standard. It was designed for lower middle-class and working families who needed accommodation costing between 30s. and £3 a month. 'Brickwork varied in colour from grey to yellow and red, and these colours were frequently used together in the decoration of porches, lintels and eaves ... The bay window on at least one floor had by now become a vogue, even in the cheapest houses, and it was here and in the construction of the porch that the distinctive embellishments of the better order of houses were concentrated. These usually took the form of plaster mouldings to make sham balustrades or unusable balconies above the bay windows, or to form tooled columns, which were often of absurdly bulky or slender dimensions. It was no rare thing for each of the capitals to these—usually composed of fossilised fruit and unidentifiable foliage—to be quite different from each of its fellows on the same house, but to be repeated (in a different permutation) a few doors away.'

In the cheaper streets 'the houses conformed to their prototype when they were first built with the mechanical fidelity of a production line'. But soon the human touches of the individual tenants appeared: 'the aspidistra, half-concealed by carefully draped lace curtains, the privet hedge of carefully determined height, the geometrical perfection of minute flower-beds edged with London Pride, the window-box trailing fern and periwinkle. . . .' These were not only expressions of individual personality, they were also an indication of the social status of the occupiers, or of that to which they aspired—an indication of their respectability.

These houses would have piped water and proper sanitation (although lavatories in many cases would be outside in the yard). Bathrooms would be rare. There would still be parts of the area without water and sewers. Gas in the 1870s and 1880s came only into the homes of the well-to-do; most people had lamps and candles, and used coal for cooking. But in 1892 the Gas Company introduced penny-in-the-slot meters, and a rent for installations, as well as making gas stoves obtainable on hire purchase, and the use of gas spread rapidly to the homes of the working class.

Further Expansion

A later suburban development was the building on adjacent fields and woods. The outer ring of suburbs had begun. Already the area around the Crystal Palace was being built up, which those who chose that new site at Sydenham Heights had considered would remain unspoiled countryside for generations to come.

The new suburbs of the later 19th century were largely the creation of the railways, but also of the very real increase in prosperity after 1873. Tax returns of the time show that middle-class incomes were increasing very rapidly. Things were better for everybody; wages either stayed the same or increased a little, while, at the same time, prices of goods and particularly of staple foods dropped substantially, sometimes as much as 25 per cent. The staples of British diet today became established, mass-produced overseas for a mass market here: New Zealand lamb and mutton and Argentine beef came in the new refrigerated ships. Though there were still small insanitary slaughter-houses in London, the great meat market of Smithfield (a splendid ironwork structure of 1868, which was built with its own railway station, now disused) handled both the overseas and the country-killed home meat. Fish poured into Billingsgate from the ports, and Covent Garden was vastly expanded. Cheese from Holland, New Zealand, fruit from Canada and America. Free Trade seemed to benefit everybody in the cities anyway, and it was particularly beneficial to that one-sixth of the nation living in London. In the 1880s, the four fastest growing areas of Great Britain were Leyton, Willesden, Tottenham and West Ham.

Willesden

Willesden in north-west London had been a mainly rural area up to 1875. There were pockets of housing, mainly villas built by City merchants at Willesden Green and Brondesbury. But with the coming of the Metropolitan Railway in 1880 people began to move into the area at the rate of one hundred a week. Closely packed residential districts close to the railway stations were built by speculative builders at a rate of over 800 new houses a year. The City merchants fled further out, and by 1895 there were almost 80,000 inhabitants in Willesden, most of them newcomers.

An excellent example of the buildings of the period can be found in Church Road, Willesden. Red brick, with the universal bow window, was favoured, particularly in the streets off this thoroughfare. Some rows of shops remain substantially unchanged. Willesden changed from inefficient Vestry rule to Local Board just in time, in 1875. Just in time, for housing shortages were so acute that several families often lived in the small two-storeyed semis which were designed for only one family, and at a pinch too if they had several children. Some speculative builders ('jerry-building' is a Victorian expression) did not even bother to connect the drains they built to the sewers! In 1894 a hospital was provided in the area for the first time, and in 1883 a school was put up which could accommodate over 8000 children.

In 1894, three free libraries were opened. By then there was an Urban District Council to co-ordinate the running of the area.

Every working father of a family, his son, and often his daughter (for 'lady typewriters' were becoming known in offices and the telephone was spreading slowly for business use in the 1890s, and needed operators) travelled into central London, into the City, the extended business districts and the West End. It was a newly improved city in which they took a pride. Was London not the biggest city in the world, capital of the greatest empire, well-paved, drained, the greatest monument to English genius?

London at the First Jubilee

June 20, 1887, fifty years to the day, since Victoria had become Queen of Great Britain and Ireland. Greater London had grown from a conglomeration of 2 million people to over 5 million. It seemed impossible that Britain's sun would ever set or that she would ever be displaced from her position as world arbiter. The queen prepared for the Jubilee celebrations that had been planned. Up went the Jubilee fountains and clocks. Twickenham had its Jubilee Avenue, the East End its Jubilee Road and Southall its Jubilee Gardens. The queen rose from her bed at Windsor Castle, drove to the station through cheering crowds and then entrained for Paddington. There was more enthusiastic cheering as she drove through the park to Buckingham Palace.

The next day she drove to the thanksgiving service at Westminster Abbey. Trafalgar Square was now completed. The lions of Landseer, Victoria's favourite animal painter, guarded Nelson on his column. In Whitehall, she passed Barry's handsome Treasury façade, and Scott's Foreign and Home Offices. She arrived at Westminster

Abbey, the north transept of which, facing Parliament Square, had been renewed by Giles Gilbert Scott and by Pearson.

The next day the queen saw 30,000 children in Hyde Park, all of whom were given a Jubilee mug and a bun. Military bands played. Later in the month she laid the foundation stone of the Imperial Institute. 'I felt dissolved by the heat, which was quite terrific,' she said, and she went on to the Albert Hall, where the RSPCA and the Battersea Dogs' Home were also celebrating the Jubilee of their sovereign. The queen had only refused to pardon one criminal in the list laid before her to celebrate her Jubilee. This was because he had been cruel to animals—'one of the worst traits in nature', wrote the queen. (She had a determined mind of her own, and would tolerate no fall from her high standards of behaviour, though she herself relaxed the rule forbidding innocent parties in a divorce action to attend court. She would have gone further if the Prime Minister had not advised against it.)

Riding in the processions of triumph were representatives from the white colonies, from India and from other parts of the Empire. The world power of Britain, with Victoria the Queen-Empress at its head, could not be denied. And this vast Empire was ruled with a tiny army. The queen, now that she had emerged from the seclusion into which she had plunged herself, was universally popular. Such upper-class Republicans as Joseph Chamberlain (born in Camberwell) and Charles Dilke (Member of Parliament for Chelsea and whose house is marked in Tite Street) became converted to Imperialism.

The Rise of Radicalism

Elsewhere, however, radical principles were stronger. In 1884 the Social Democratic Federation was founded, a high-sounding body with no grass-roots support, but theoretically Marxist. William Morris became a member, as did other well-known intellectuals. The headquarters of another radical club of the time still stands, at 37A Clerkenwell Green, E.C.1; it is now the Marx Memorial Library. The building itself dates from 1730, but in the 1880s it was the meeting-place of the Patriotic Club, many of whom were socialists. At the same time the Fabian Society was formed; this was a body of middle-class intellectuals, who advocated the slow, gradual but complete transformation of society until a socialist basis was reached.

The principal political parties were also active, for universal manhood suffrage had, for all practical purposes, been achieved in 1884. London became littered with 'Constitutional' and Conservative clubs, and Liberal or 'Radical' clubs. The great Pall Mall political clubs like the Reform for the Liberals and the Carlton for the Tories, belonged to an earlier day, the 1840s or so, and they were for MPs and well-off party chieftains. They now had their counterpart on a more humble level.

By this time, too, there were organised Trade Unions, though they were mostly for skilled workers, and were most heavily supported in the heavy engineering industries of the North and Midlands. It was in London that the unskilled workers first made their protests heard.

There were great popular demonstrations in Trafalgar Square—one of which was dramatically cleared by a charge of the Household Cavalry—and then the Great Dock Strike of 1889 came, demanding 6d. an hour and regular employment. The strike lasted six weeks, enjoyed universal support, and was successful. The Match Girls at Bryant and May's factory in Fairfield Road, E.3 went on strike. It is worth a visit as an example of a model factory of the time; but most match girls were not as fortunate as those that worked there.

So the East End won victories in the struggle to improve working conditions. Such victories were sorely needed. In this immensely crowded area much industry was carried on in small sweat-shops. Of the population of the area, 40 per cent were engaged in manufacturing industry (for the rest of London the figure was 25 per cent). Most were in some sort of clothing industry: tailoring, shirt-making or boot-making or in processing furs and leather. Others were employed making furniture or specialist instruments, book-binding and so on.

Clothes and cleaning

The Jews had come into the tailoring trade, mainly from Poland and Russia. The 1880s saw a great advance in retailing and the mass-production of clothes. The Jewish tailors were able, by simplifying the cut of garments and by using machines, to compete in the mass market, while the traditional bespoke English tailors could not. Before this time there was no dry-cleaning, and all garments were first sponged, and then, as they grew dirty and sweat-stained, picked apart at the seams, washed, and fitted together again. Upper and middle-class households with masses of servants could do this if they wished, and if the master was a dandy, such cleaned clothes could always be given to the servants. But the poor could not afford such clothes in the first place or to have them cleaned by such a complicated process. They usually wore second-hand clothes.

This is why workers in Victorian photographs or drawings always look so crumpled. They also undoubtedly smelled. There were no deodorants and the very poorest slept in their day clothes. The obsession of the later Victorians with hygiene is understandable, and soap advertising from the mid-70s onward approached modern detergent 'wars' and surpassed even them in daring. The 'give-away offer' was pioneered, all kinds of claims made; Queen Victoria herself was often depicted using the advertised product.

*Typical wear for a gentleman in the 1850s. Later in the century,
mass-produced clothes and dry-cleaning raised the general standard
of dress.*

94

The Jewish immigrants who came into the East End from Russia after the persecutions of 1881—and indeed from all parts of Europe—congregated in Whitechapel. In this area of less than one square mile there were nearly 40,000 Jews. Yiddish was the language of the streets: everywhere there were signs in Hebrew. There was dense overcrowding. The percentage of persons per acre rose to 227, the highest in the East End. So London had a ghetto. The Jewish tailors would make a jacket for 5d., the most expensive bespoke morning coat for 12s.

Working-class Housing

The general crowding not only in Whitechapel but in the whole of the East End led quite early in the period to the building of blocks of 'model' dwellings for the working class. One of the earliest benefactors of the area was the Baroness Burdett Coutts, who put up Columbia Square, a great Gothic square of tenements in Bethnal Green in 1859. (Next to it she also built a vast Gothic market, but this has been demolished.) Another benefactor was George Peabody, a generous American businessman, who gave £400,000 to the London poor. Peabody Buildings can be found in Westminster, Bermondsey and Southwark as well as the East End, where the earliest example is in Commercial Street, Stepney. Large blocks of buildings were also put up by such bodies as the East End Dwellings Company. In the 'buildings' there were of course no lifts, but landings and staircases, which, in the earlier examples, are dark and airless; later they were better lit. Baths were installed in the basements, but water had to be heated up and carried down to them, so that most tenants preferred to use the public baths, with which most districts were well provided.

The Metropolitan Board of Works, which in its short life built so much of modern London, was replaced by the London County Council in 1888. This change was

Peabody Square, Westminster, one of the working-class housing schemes endowed by the American philanthropist George Peabody.

part of a nation-wide rationalisation of local government. From 1894 the local vestries were replaced with more powerful local bodies. Both these and the LCC had a whole host of new powers granted to them by Acts of Parliament. Among these powers were those created by the Housing of the Working Classes Act 1890; from then on, local authorities could build dwellings to house poorer people.

The first borough-built flats were in Nile Street, Shoreditch, put up in 1896–99. They looked a lot more pleasant than the charitable trust housing, and were designed and put up by an authority on the housing of the working classes, Rowland Plumbe; they even had electric light. The LCC also put up its first flats at this time (1897–1900), some in Kensington, others in Boundary Street Estate, Bethnal Green.

Education

At first, however, the LCC did not gain control over education; nor did the local authorities. This responsibility was in the hands of the London School Board, a specially elected body chosen by all the ratepayers of London to supervise elementary education and to build the appropriate schools. These old Board Schools are scattered all over the metropolis, three or four storeys high, and towering above their neighbouring terraces of modest houses. Examples can be seen in Warner Street, off the Gray's Inn Road or Messina Road, N.W.6. Many have been converted into evening institutes.

At first, from 1870, school fees were charged; the average fee was 10s. a year and parents were punishable by law if they did not provide this 'education tax'. (Pauper children had separate provision made for them.) From 1876, it was established as a general principle that no child under ten should be employed, as this would interfere with his education.

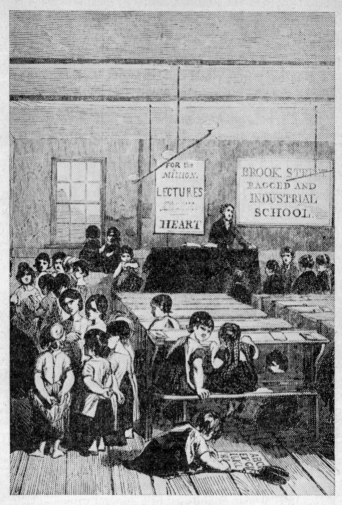

A classroom in a 'ragged school', supported by charity for pauper children. After the Education Act 1870, all public primary schooling came under the control of the London School Board.

From 1891, with a fresh Act of Parliament, the London School Board ceased to charge school fees. Gradually, too, the voluntary schools, the religious and 'Ragged Schools' transferred their establishments to the Board, which usually built a new school to house the children.

Workhouses

The poor and destitute who were unlucky enough to have to throw themselves on public charity were still, at the end of the century, liable to the provisions of the Poor Law, which was specifically designed to make public institutions as uncomfortable as possible. There were workhouses in each part of London, administered by a Board of Guardians, elected by members of a parish or a number of parishes. Examples of workhouses still standing, though now used for other purposes, can be found in Poplar High Street and in Ladywell Road, Lewisham.

On admission to the workhouse, according to a guide to London's government in 1898, 'the applicant is examined by the medical officer, is made to bathe, is deprived of his or her clothes and possessions, which are detained and only given up in the event of discharge, is clothed in a workhouse dress, and is sent to the proper ward'. Husbands were separated from wives, and parents from children. Casual paupers, applying for a night's lodging, were not in for a soft time either: 'In return for food and shelter for one night the casual has to perform a task which, in the case of men consists in: The breaking of two cwt of stones . . . ; or three hours' work in washing, scrubbing or cleaning; or the picking of half-a-pound of unbeaten or one pound of beaten oakum.' The food provided was also of the most meagre description, consisting of six ounces of bread and one pint of gruel or one pint of broth for supper, and the same for breakfast.

The Naughty Nineties

London relaxed in the last decade of the 19th century. The stresses of moving from a developing to a mature industrial society had been triumphantly surmounted. There had been some terrible mistakes, but the cities to come could learn from London, the pioneer in the art of living in megalopolis.

Entertainment

As prosperity became more widespread, life became less earnest. It was the golden age of the music-hall. Marie Lloyd, George Robey, Dan Leno, Little Titch, and Albert Chevalier were all London-born and they made this popular entertainment essentially the cockney's own. We still remember 'My Old Dutch', and 'Knocked 'em in the Old Kent Road', which were the songs of Albert Chevalier, 'Any Old Iron', from Harry Champion, 'Don't Dilly Dally', from Marie Lloyd, and 'Two Lovely Black Eyes', from Charles Coburn. Celebrities of the day also included Blondin, the tightrope-walker, Captain Webb, the Channel swimmer, and the German strongman Eugene Sandow, who lifted unbelievable weights.

The music-halls reflected the intense patriotism of the people. Any appearance of the Union Jack would be the signal for the whole house to break into (often slightly beery) cheering. 'The Union Jack of Dear Old England' would always bring the house down; so would 'Tommy, Tommy Atkins', and of course 'Soldiers of the Queen' would provoke a frenzy of enthusiasm when the British were fighting the Boers (which they seemed to be doing, or about to do, all through the 1880s and 1890s).

There were great music-halls in the centre of London, of which the best-known were perhaps the Alhambra, and the Empire in Leicester Square. These theatres had 'promenades', as did many others, where patrons could walk up and down, admire each other, and approach good-looking girls for dates after the show. When an attempt was made by a self-appointed suppressor of vice, Mrs. Ormiston Chant, and members of the LCC to separate the bars at the Empire from the promenade where the ladies of the town touted for trade, Winston Churchill, then a Sandhurst cadet, flew to the defence of the freedom of the individual. In his first letter to a national newspaper in 1894, he thundered 'in England we have too long obeyed the voice of the prude'. After the partition at the Empire had been erected, he headed a mob of three hundred who stormed the barricade and tore it down.

Entertainments, particularly at the Alhambra, were most elaborately staged. At the Alhambra the first successful film was shown in 1896. It was a film of the Derby, won by the Prince of Wales's horse Persimmon; it was greeted with wild enthusiasm, the audience demanding that the film should be repeated over and over again. Films gradually increased in length, but were still only shorts by modern standards; the first cinema in London was not opened until Edwardian days.

The 'legitimate' theatre was also flourishing. Arthur Pinero was the fashionable playwright of the early 90s.

He wrote mostly about and for the West End audience—what he called 'our parish of St. James'. His play *The Second Mrs. Tanqueray* (1892) dealt with high society, but with a novel twist—the lady was a fallen woman. 1892 also saw a play of more direct social protest, *Widower's Houses*, Bernard Shaw's first play to be produced, which exposed the misdemeanours of absentee landlords.

The Aesthetic Movement

This was also the year of *Lady Windermere's Fan*, in which Oscar Wilde made his debut as a dramatist. Already renowned as a wit, a writer, a poet, the most extraordinary man in fashionable London—his dress was strange and unmistakable—he now showed that he was a master of the stage. Wilde, in his person and his writing, represents the antithesis of all that is thought of as Victorian. He was mocking, irreverent, satirical, and immensely funny. He professed to be a socialist (though his political ideas were not a thing he paid much attention to). He stated that all that mattered in the world was art, and that there was no such thing as 'good' art or 'bad' art; art was not a matter for morality. What mattered was whether a thing was done well, and whether it succeeded as an artistic venture. In the 1880s he was at the hub of the Aesthetic Movement (parodied by Gilbert and Sullivan, in *Patience*), of which Chelsea and South Kensington became the centre.

The tendency among this small but fashionable coterie was to admire the style of the Japanese, to place a single sunflower or lily in a slender pot, and to have furniture which, in contrast to the bulbous mahogany of the prosperous middle-class merchant, was slim, spiky, and probably made of bamboo. Designs were simplified.

A whole quarter of London was laid out in an architectural style much favoured by the aesthetes. Go to

Hans Place and Cadogan Gardens and see a curious array of house façades, most of them in terracotta. This is the 'Queen Anne' or 'Pont Street Dutch' style. Cadogan Square includes houses by Norman Shaw, the best architect of this style, and indeed the acknowledged creator of it. Look at Nos. 72, 68 and 60a. On the Chelsea Embankment, you can see examples of his work at No. 17, Swan House (1875), Nos. 11 to 9, and also Cheyne House.

Nearby in Tite Street lived many of the principal artists of London of the 1870s, 80s and 90s. Whistler, Wilde's great rival in wit, lived in the extraordinary White House, built for him in 1879. This, No. 33 and the Tower House on the other side of the street were designed by Edward Godwin.

Wilde was associated with *The Yellow Book,* a monthly magazine with very advanced contributors, including Aubrey Beardsley, the young consumptive artist whose drawings have a strange, compulsive and unhealthy power. The movement was labelled 'decadent', and many of the circle gloried in this name, since it distinguished them from the rest of society. Wilde was a sort of hippy verging on middle age—he was in his forties in 1895—who thought most of his contemporaries hopelessly square. Many of the circle took drugs, or drank absinthe, which was just as destructive to the physique.

The Yellow Book had a flavour of art nouveau about it. This style, which was the international vogue of the late 90s, owes much to English decorative design, especially the wallpaper designs of Walter Crane and A. H. Mackmurdo. All was sinuous, attenuated and elaborate. It provided different 'intervals', proportion and shape from earlier styles. The rules of classical or Gothic architecture, which the Victorians loved, were discarded. In domestic architecture, Charles Voysey's house at 14 South Parade, Bedford Park (1891), is a very early example of the 'different proportions' effect, though it is not characteristically art nouveau in its decorative

*Vagrants in the casual ward of a workhouse. Workhouses were
extremely forbidding, accommodating only the most destitute and
most desperate.*

treatment; indeed, decoration is conspicuously absent.

Other examples of this new trend in architecture can be found in the houses put up by C. R. Ashbee in Cheyne Walk; no. 37 was built in 1894. A word of warning, however: nos. 38–39, the most typically art nouveau, date in fact from 1904. The Mary Ward Settlement in Tavistock Place (1895), the Whitechapel Art Gallery (1897) and the Horniman Museum, Forest Hill, Lewisham (1900) should also be looked at.

By the end of the century, even fashionable people began to live in blocks of flats. The first to be completed was designed by Norman Shaw: Albert Hall mansions, built in 1879. However, the first block to be begun was Queen Anne Mansions in Petty France. From the start it had hydraulic lifts. Queen Anne Mansions is perhaps the ugliest building in Westminster; it should have been higher, but it is said that Queen Victoria objected to being overlooked by subjects when she was being wheeled around the gardens of Buckingham Palace.

All this building, all this continual urbanisation, went on in a London that was still crammed with animals —horses for buses, donkeys for the costermongers' carts; there were even sheep. According to an account of 1893, a curious custom took place every year in an enclosure at the south-west corner of Kensington Palace: 'This is the annual sheep-shearing. Thousands of sheep are brought from Scotland and distributed over London wherever grazing can be obtained. After the shearing, the sheep are kept awhile in the park for fattening, and thence gradually find their way to the butchers' shops.'

In 1894 the Victorians added another potent symbol of London to the capital's skyline—Tower Bridge. Built as a bascule bridge to permit access by shipping to the heart of the city, it immediately became one of the sights of the capital. It is still worked by the same hydraulic system installed when it was first opened. Permission to view the machinery should be sought from the Captain of the Bridge; to see the Bridge in action at close quarters is an impressive sight.

Travel

In the last year of the 19th century the last of the London main-line termini was built—Marylebone station—a charming, genteel building, looking as though it has strayed from Cadogan Place. It was the terminus for the Great Central, which was not a prosperous railway, as one might expect of a line that only arrived in 1899 and then only over the Metropolitan line from Willesden.

Generally, it became easier to travel about London as new methods of public transport were introduced. In the late 1880s there were steam trams on the roads of London, but these were withdrawn in 1890. There were also cable-drawn trams, including the London Tramways line from Kennington to Streatham—which was very useful for getting up Brixton Hill. Electric trams did not appear before 1900, but before then petrol buses were running in very small numbers on the roads.

Electricity was also used for the very first deep tube. This was a major engineering feat in every sense; it was a tremendously imaginative and technically brilliant scheme. The first successful project was for a tube (so-called because trains run through an iron tube, constructed deep down) to run from the Monument to the Elephant and Castle. This was authorised by Parliament in 1884. At first it was planned to draw the carriages by cable. Then the railway was to be extended to Stockwell. It was decided to use electric traction (by locomotives, and not, as on today's Underground, by motors attached directly to the carriages).

On November 4, 1890, the City and South London Railway was officially opened by the Prince of Wales, and public services began on December 18. There was only one class (unlike the Inner Circle of the time) and only one price, 2d. You can see one of the original locomotives in the Science Museum. Another tube of the 1890s was the Waterloo & City (still running in the hands of British Rail) and then came the great leap forward in tube construction with the Central London.

Increasing mobility made West End shops accessible not only to the fashionable, but to the suburbanites. The Oxford Street stores expanded. The great shop of the period was Whiteley's in Westbourne Grove, the 'Universal Provider'. Special buses ran to the store—in 1885 more than 700 a day—and for a time the store actually ran a bus service of its own to Maida Vale. For a shop front of the period, Smith's the Umbrella Shop at 32 New Oxford Street is a good example.

Another development in shopping after 1870 was the growth of chain stores, not only in London but all over the country; branches of Lipton's, Sainsbury's, an old-established London firm, and the Home and Colonial sprang up in suburban high streets.

Sport

Sport also became more popular in the 80s and 90s, both to participate in and to watch. Previously sport had been mostly for the middle classes. Cricket was not for the London slum-dweller and the crazes of earlier decades, such as croquet in the 60s and roller-skating in the 70s (much condemned, as young men would twine their arms around girls' waists, ostensibly to give them support), were also confined to the middle class. But the fashion for bicycling was one which could be enjoyed by anyone who could afford a machine, which could pay for itself in the fares saved, if ridden to work. There were soon millions of bicycles, and the big firms all opened offices on Holborn Viaduct. Gymnastics, swimming and physical culture were all quite popular. Parks—such as Hyde

Peter Robinson in Oxford Circus in 1891. Easier travel brought an enormous increase in custom to the West End department stores.

Park, Regent's Park and Victoria Park—had rowing boats for hire. In the summer visitors could explore the higher reaches of the Thames, Richmond, Boulter's Lock, which a cheap-day return ticket made easily accessible. Visits were paid to the museums at South Kensington and to the great national sporting events, such as the first Test Matches and the Derby. Olympia was opened in 1886, Earl's Court was a pleasure ground from 1894 and had a giant Great Wheel as a special attraction. Barnum's circus was at Olympia in the winter of 1889, but by 1890 a more popular revival of roller skating turned it into a huge rink.

All over London were branches of W. H. Smith, and like all other newsagents, they sold the products of Fleet Street, which now became the acknowledged centre of the newspaper industry. (The smaller provincial papers which maintain offices there are often still housed in their original buildings.) Popular newspapers had arrived, including W. T. Stead's *Pall Mall Gazette* (he was the editor 1883–89), George Newnes's *Tit-bits*, and the Harmsworth Brothers' *Answers* and *Comic Cuts*, this last for children. In 1894 the Harmsworths bought the *Evening News*, and in 1896 they launched the *Daily Mail*, which, at a price of ½d, had reached a circulation of half a million copies, twice as much as any other paper, at the end of the century.

The London skyline, with all its new buildings, was not entirely elegant. Advertisements, called sky-signs, were erected on grids and poles on the roofs of any building whose proprietors would have them. They were lit at night, often spelling their message in the 1890s with hundreds of electric light bulbs. This mad, alpha-betical jungle on the skyline was eventually banned. Another sign of progress that could be seen on gazing upwards were the masts and cross-bars that held tele-graph, and later telephone, wires. We now put all these underground. But, however brash advertisements might

be—and they shouted from every available hoarding—
they reflected the commercial bustle and energy of this
great city, making money, a magnet for business, and
for every other, talent.

Postscript: 1900

London in 1900 was the capital of a nation at war. True,
by today's standards there was little sign of it. There
were more troops in the streets than usual, and they
were now in khaki. You might see a boy cyclist pedalling
furiously amongst the traffic, in a khaki uniform, sporting
a red sash with the words 'Bovril War Cables'. Bovril ran,
as an advertising gimmick, a service which took the latest
information to selected shops. News of the war was also
pinned up outside the Mansion House. Britain was fighting the Boers again. Most foreign countries admired this
'gallant little nation', which was standing up to the
British colossus. The street organs and German bands
played 'Goodbye Dolly I must leave you'—one of the
hits of 1900. It might be heard on one of the Edison-Bell
phonographs, which were now becoming quite popular
for those who could afford two guineas and the cost of
the cylindrical wax records. It was heard as the City
Imperial Volunteers, in their khaki topees, marched
through the streets and past the Lord Mayor to take their
chance in South Africa.

Traffic of this great city was still drawn by thousands
of horses. In and out among the vehicles darted boys
with pans and brushes; the precious droppings would be
sold to fertilise suburban gardens. There were crossing-
sweepers too, who kept a path across the road clear, and
expected to be tipped by gentlemen. These last were
easy to distinguish. First, there was the top hat; then the
frock or morning coat, meticulously cut, the white waist-
coat, the cravat with its jewelled pin, the starched collar
and cuffs, the slim cane. Lesser mortals wore bowlers;

workmen wore caps. There were numerous class 'uniforms', which were easily distinguished. Servants wore livery of some kind. A lady was always recognisable as such—partly by very rarely being seen in the streets alone. She would either have an escorting male, some female friend, or a servant with her. Private carriages, many in the livery and armorial bearings of their owners, appeared in the traffic, with coachman and footman 'on the box'. In this city of 4½ million people half a million households had servants, who numbered about 210,000—that is, servants who lived in. If we were to count the 'dailies' and the people who served in shops and hotels, a very large proportion of London's population would seem to be looking after the rest.

It was said that motor cars 'were something of a surprise packet even in the streets of London in 1900'. There were only four petrol 'stockists'. The Prince of Wales adored motoring—he rather liked anything fast—and bought the first royal Daimler in 1900. As for public transport, motor omnibuses (fare ½d) were now running from the Polytechnic via Oxford Circus, Regent's Park, Piccadilly Circus, Charing Cross, Westminster Bridge, and Kennington Road, to Kennington Park.

Cabs were of two kinds: the four-wheeler, which took four people and a fifth if necessary on top, and the two-wheeled hansom, for two people. These 'gondolas of London', as Disraeli called them, were fast and elegant, and much used. There had also been a small number of electric cabs on the road since 1897. There were over 11,000 cabs altogether, employing 20,000 horses. On special occasions, those without a carriage could hire a 'fly'. These had to be ordered in advance from the local livery stable. The Coupé and Dunlop Brougham Company of Regent Street hired out its smart flys at 7s. 6d. for the first two hours.

The Central London Railway—today's Central Line—was operating from Shepherd's Bush to the Bank. It was one of the sights of the year, celebrated as the '2d. tube', and it was an immediate success.

As for telephones, 'the telephonic communication of London is mainly in the hands of the National Telephone Company; there are numerous call-rooms throughout London and district, open to the public at the rate of 3d for each three minutes conversation'. It had been possible to speak to Paris since 1891.

There were also conveniences which we have lost. The Corps of Commissionaries would carry parcels for you. There was a District Messenger Service, and companies delivered parcels to your home from numerous receiving offices. You simply went in with your parcel and they did the rest; lines of carriers' vehicles went over London with almost the regularity of the bus routes. Service was available at every turn, for this was a society rich in labour and dozens of pairs of hands were always available to help—particularly if you had the means. In some districts, there were actually twelve deliveries of letters a day!

There were fifty music-halls and fifty theatres. Some 325,000 people went to them every night, a total attendance of about 100 million a year. Copies of the play were often sold at the theatre. The London Season was the best time for visitors. Then the greatest artistes in the world were performing at the opera.

But the season was not only for going to the opera. The fashionable went there mostly to be seen. Foreigners, in particular Americans, attempted to enter the exclusive society of the English leisured class. The royal road was through presentation at court, presided over by the Prince of Wales now that the queen was feeling her age. Unmarried ladies wore two ostrich feathers in their hair, married ladies, three.

The Death of Victoria

Victoria was now in her eighties; it was difficult for her

A prospective passenger hails a hansom cab. Two-wheeled hansoms were popular and plentiful; in 1897 there were over 11,000 cabs in London.

The uniforms of letter carriers, mail guards and drivers employed by the Post Office in December 1860. The 'Penny Post', established in 1849, helped to revolutionise communications.

to read, and letters were written in larger and larger script for her. In this last year of her life the old lady pushed herself hard. Her troops were fighting in South Africa, and the Queen-Empress would not let them down. When British troops had been forced to surrender in 1899 the Prime Minister's nephew Balfour was told: 'Please understand that there is no-one depressed in this house; we are not interested in the possibilities of defeat; they do not exist.'

Her confidence was justified. Ladysmith was relieved. Two triumphal drives were made through the streets of London, the demonstrations at which surpassed those of the two Jubilees. Crowds poured on to the London streets with even greater enthusiasm when Mafeking, with Baden-Powell inside, was relieved. Everything in London stopped for the night of May 15, 1900, as people went mad with excitement. From then on the old queen's health steadily deteriorated. The next year she died at Osborne House, in the Isle of Wight; for ten days she lay there in state, and then her body was brought to London.

She had ordered that there should be no black hangings in the London streets on that day in February, 1901. They were to be hung with purple instead. The gun carriage bore the body from Victoria to Paddington station, on its way to Windsor. Victoria had left the capital for ever. She had presided symbolically over its greatest transformation. She believed in improvement, and the city had progressed immeasurably since she had driven to her coronation in 1837.

Museums to Visit

British Museum

Address: Great Russell Street, W.C.1
Admission: Free
Opening hours: Monday—Saturday: 10 am—5 pm
                Sunday: 2.30 pm—6 pm
Closed: Christmas Day and Good Friday
                Open Bank Holidays usual hours

Access:

By Underground:

Tottenham Court Road (Central & Northern Lines)—turn right along Tottenham Court Road and right at Great Russell Street. Museum on left.

Russell Square (Piccadilly Line)—left out of station, cross Russell Square, and left on Montague Street to Great Russell Street and main entrance of Museum.

By Bus:

77, 68, 188, 196, to Southampton Row. Turn left along Great Russell Street.

73, to Tottenham Court Road/Oxford Street. Right along Great Russell Street.

7, 8, 23, 25, to Bloomsbury Way. Turn along Museum Street (from West).

7, 8, 22, 23, 25, from Holborn direction. Alight at High Holborn, just past Kingsway, and cross road, along Drury Lane or Grape Street, cross New Oxford Street and continue along Coptic Street or Museum Street.

116

By Car:

Drive from West along Oxford Street, turn left at Tottenham Court Road, and right almost immediately at Great Russell Street.

From East, along Holborn to Kingsway, turn right along Southampton Row, and left at Great Russell Street.

N.B. There is limited parking at the Museum—otherwise, at side in Montague Street/Russell Square.

Bethnal Green Museum

Address :	Cambridge Heath Road, London, E.2
Admission :	Free
Opening hours :	Weekdays : 10 am—6 pm
	Sundays : 2.30 pm—6 pm
Closed :	Good Friday, Christmas Day

Access :

By Underground:

Bethnal Green Station.

By Bus:

8, 8a, 106, 253.

By Train:

Cambridge Heath Station (all lines from Liverpool Street Station).

Cuming Museum

Address: Above Library next to Town Hall,
                      Walworth Road, Southwark, S.E.17
Admission: Free
Opening hours: Opens Monday—Saturday: 10 am
                      Closes at 5.30 pm except Thursday at
                      7 pm. Saturday at 5 pm
Closed: Sundays, Bank Holidays, and Holy
                      Days

Access:

By Underground:

Elephant & Castle (Bakerloo & Northern Lines)—out of station, cross Newington Butts, bear right, round traffic circuits to Walworth Road on left. About 300 yards along on left.

By Bus:

12, 17, 35, 40A, 45, to Museum. Ask for Town Hall, Walworth Road.

By Car:

Aim at Elephant and Castle which is well signposted. Drive round traffic circuit and bear left at Walworth Road, direction Camberwell. Museum on left about 300 yards along. Park in side streets.

Guildhall Museum

Address :	On Bassishaw High Walk, up stairs by Gillette House in Basinghall Street, overlooking London Wall, E.C.2
Admission :	Free
Opening hours :	Monday—Saturday : 10 am—5 pm
Closed :	Sundays, Bank Holidays, Holy Days— e.g. Christmas and Good Friday

Access :

By Underground :

Aldersgate (Metropolitan or Circle Lines)—turn right out of station along Aldersgate as far as London Wall. Turn left—Museum up on high walk-way opposite ruin of church tower.

St. Paul's (Central Line)—walk along Cheapside to Wood Street, left to Gresham Street, right for one block to Aldermanbury. Up stairs on right at end before junction with London Wall.

Moorgate (Metropolitan & Northern Lines)—turn right along Moorgate to London Wall. Turn left.

Bank (Central Line)—along Princes Street at side of Bank of England to Gresham Street. Left as far as Basinghall Street. Right. Museum at far end of Basinghall Street up steps by Gillette House.

By Bus :

7, 8, 22, 23, 25, to St. Paul's end of Cheapside, then follow instructions given under St. Paul's Underground Station above.

76, 43, 21, 11, 9, 141, to London Wall/Moorgate. Follow instructions as from Moorgate Station.

By Car:

Parking is difficult except at weekends out of 'meter' hours. No parking at any time on London Wall.

From East: drive to the Bank then along Princes Street by Bank of England, turn left at Gresham Street, and right at Aldermanbury.

From West: Holborn/Newgate Street turn left at Aldersgate and right at Gresham Street. Park in area behind Guildhall.

Geffrye Museum

Address :   Kingsland Road, Shoreditch, E.2
Admission :   Free
Opening hours :   Tuesday—Saturday 10 am—5 pm
                    Sunday : 2 pm—5 pm
Closed :   Mondays, except Bank Holidays,
                    Christmas Day

Access :

By Underground:
Liverpool Street (Metropolitan and Central London Lines)
and Old Street (Northern).

By Bus:
22, 35, 36, 47, 67, 78, 149, 170, 243, 256, 257. Alight at
Kingsland Road (Pearson Street request stop).

Museum of British Transport, Clapham

Address :   The Triangle, Clapham High
                    Street, S.W.4
Admission :   5s.
Opening hours :   10 am—5.30 pm weekdays only

Access :

By Underground:
Clapham Common (Northern Line).

By Bus:
88, 155.

London Museum

Address :   Kensington Palace,
                            Kensington Gardens, W.8

Admission :   Free

Opening hours :   1 March—30 September :
                            10 am—6 pm (Sundays : 2 pm—6 pm)
                            1 October—28 February :
                            10 am—4 pm (Sundays : 2 pm—4 pm)

Closed :   Good Friday, Christmas Eve, and
                            Christmas Day

Access :

By Underground :

Queensway (Central Line)—cross Bayswater Road and walk through Broad Walk in Kensington Gardens to Palace.
Kensington High Street (Circle & District Line from Earl's Court to Edgware Road)—turn right along Kensington High Street to Park. Left through Park to Palace.

By Bus :

12, 88, along Bayswater Road to Queensway, then as above from Queensway Station.

9, 46, 52, 73, to Palace Gate in Kensington Road. Walk through Park to Palace.

By Car :

The best place to park is in the squares and side streets off Bayswater Road or Kensington Road. Then walk through Park.

Victoria and Albert Museum

Address: South Kensington, S.W.7

Admission: Free

Opening hours: Monday—Saturday: 10 am—6 pm

                Sunday: 2.30 pm—6 pm

Closed: Christmas Day and Good Friday

                Open Bank Holidays usual hours

Access:

By Underground:

South Kensington (District, Circle and Piccadilly Lines) —a subway connects the station and the museum, giving entrance on N.W. (Exhibition Road) side. Main entrance to museum is on Cromwell Road.

By Bus:

207, 45, 49, to South Kensington Station.

14, 30, 74, to Brompton Oratory, at junction of Brompton Road and Cromwell Road.

Further reading list

Winslow Ames	*Prince Albert and Victorian Taste,* Chapman & Hall
T. C. Barker Michael Robbins	*A History of London Transport* (vol i), George Allen & Unwin
Charles Booth	*Life and Labour of the People,* Macmillan
G. F. Chadwick	*The Works of Sir Joseph Paxton,* Architectural Press
John R. Day	*The Story of London's Underground,* London Transport
H. J. Dyos	*Victorian Suburb,* University of Leicester Press
P. J. Edwards	*History of London Street Improvements,* London County Council
Geoffrey Fletcher	*The London Nobody Knows,* Penguin Books
R. Furneaux Jordan	*Victorian Architecture,* Penguin Books
Henry Jephson	*The Sanitary Evolution of London,* George Allen & Unwin
Osbert Lancaster	*Here of All Places,* John Murray
Elizabeth Longford	*Victoria R. I.,* Weidenfeld & Nicolson
Henry Mayhew	*London Labour and the London Poor,* Griffen, Bohn & Co.
Nikolaus Pevsner	*Buildings of England: London* (vols i and ii), Penguin Books
E. R. Pike	*Human Documents of the Victorian Golden Age,* George Allen & Unwin

R. M. Rayner	*Recent Times, 1868–*, Longmans, Green
Frederick Whelen	*London Government*, Grant Richards
Aubrey Wilson	*London's Industrial Heritage*, David & Charles

Discovering London

Other Books in the Series

This volume is one of a set of eight books that trace the growth of London from Roman times to the end of Queen Victoria's reign. The other books are:

Set One

1. *Roman London* by Grace Derwent
2. *The Conqueror's London* by Derek Brechin
3. *Medieval London* by Kenneth Derwent
4. *Tudor London* by A. G. Robertson

Set Two

5. *Stuart London* by Malpas Pearse
6. *Georgian London* by Derek Brechin
7. *Regency London* by Douglas Hill
8. This book

Each title is available separately, price 5s. Alternatively each set of four volumes is available in box with a special fold-out map of the area, price 21s.